With this book, T̶ dares to
At the beginning of the twenty-first
century, most celebrated examples of
architecture are unavoidably spectacular.
Unimaginable cantilevers, rotating towers,
gigantic cupolas and exuberant shapes are
features without which the contemporary
building will hardly be registered in the
skyline or the media. Unequivocally, the
buildings getting attention are the iconic
ones. Never before has architecture tried so
hard to amaze. But are these icons true
celebrations of human achievements?
Taking a critical stance towards the global
production of the spectacular, The Why
Factory investigates the future of
amazement in architecture. What
constitutes a 'world wonder' today? How
can we provoke wonder and what can we
wonder about, now that almost nothing
is impossible in architecture?
This book contemplates the wonders of the
ancient and modern world, and innocently
explores new questions and
their fantastications.

*We Want World Wonders* by The Why Factory:
Winy Maas and Tihamér Salij

# Table of Contents

# Do We Need New Architectural Myths?
## Epilogue
Tihamér Salij

# We Want World Wonders.

## Introduction

Winy Maas

The Pyramids of Giza, the Hanging Gardens of Babylon, the Eiffel Tower and recently maybe the Millau Viaduct are structures that, as their reputations indicate, seem to play a role on the planetary scale. They are somehow valuable to many people – we love them. They thus could be seen as the most sustainable buildings ever made . . .

It's a fascinating realm. Don't all architects, children, politicians, leaders and clients dream of making such a wonder? So how do we make them? Don't we all want to know under what conditions they can appear?

These are buildings that are surrounded by stories, by myths. Impossible, heroic works on superlative scales. And often the visions of insane commissioners.

Such buildings make us wonder. And they make us think. They impress us and thus somehow guide us.

They put our daily lives and efforts into perspective, and maybe that is why they comfort us. They have something that goes beyond our usual surroundings and initial imagination. They enter into the zone of myths themselves and, ultimately, of divinity.

They are a sign of the times.

Building activities are limited in economically vulnerable, uncertain and nervous times, and repurposing may be the only useful activity left. Perhaps small structures are being built here and there, but in times such as the current ones, everything seems to focus on survival and downsizing. And in times such as these, when slums all over the planet are actually growing and the chasm between rich and poor is getting wider and wider, thinking big seems to be an insane taboo.

Are we still allowed to dream about wonders? Are we still allowed to make world wonders?

Of course we are.

But we all know that any world problem deserves a solution. . Maybe a world wonder is revived when it tackles these problems. It can create a new purpose for architectural and urbanist agendas. And so: food producers, energy generators, poverty eradicators, climate modifiers – these could be the new world wonders.

Anyway,  the drive to be the best is existential. Isn't there always a hidden desire or drive to 'surpass' the past as a means of achieving visibility, in an ongoing Darwinian battle for superlatives? As in sports, the drive to beat the highest, the longest, the smallest, the nicest and the best is always present, also (or maybe even especially) in unexpected situations, due to unexpected demands.

And besides that, the eagerness to exploit and know the unknown seems to be supremely human. Aren't there always clients and institutions that strive for the unknown? Isn't there always a place for curiosity?

And aren't there always necessities that demand innovations that at first glance seem insane? Are innovations not some of the most intriguing corners of our existence?

Let's explore this world of wonders and wonderment. Let's examine current classifications. And let's wonder about new categories. Let's speculate through the eyes of architecture students about the possible fields that can push us towards the realization of new world wonders, of exemplary and wonderful projects. Let's create a new atlas of wonders . . .

# Is There a Desire for World Wonders?

Tihamér Salij

'In my travels I found no answers, only wonders.'

Marty Rubin (American writer and journalist, 1930-1994)

# Lists of World Wonders

Man-made world wonders have marked our past civilizations and continue to dominate and fascinate us. From the Great Pyramid of Giza to the Colosseum in Rome, from the Great Wall of China to the Eiffel Tower – man-made world wonders have been driven by individual dreams and desires, beauty, myth, universal values and, of course, the politics, philosophy, economy and technological limitations of their time. All embody a fascination with the exceptional, the beautiful, and especially with the inexplicable, magical and mysterious. Many authors – from Antipater of Sidon and Fischer von Erlach to Deborah Cadbury with the BBC – have produced lists of their favourite man-made wonders, lists with contents that reflect the essence of human existence – our emotions, vanities and aspirations as well as our humility, fears and mortality.

# Ancient Wonders

In the second century BC, ancient Greek poet Antipater of Sidon listed seven marvels of his time, as did other Greek scholars such as Philo of Byzantium, Herodotus, Diodorus of Sicily and Strabo. There were seven wonders, because in ancient times the number 7 was considered to be divine and represented the idea of the universe. This list was meant as a guide for Hellenic travellers to give them access to the influential Egyptian, Persian and Babylonian cultures of their time.

The Seven Wonders of the Ancient World are the Great Pyramid of Giza, the Hanging Gardens of Babylon, the Statue of Zeus, the Temple of Artemis at Ephesus, the Mausoleum at Halicarnassus, the Colossus of Rhodes and the Lighthouse of Alexandria.

They were built for various reasons: the Pyramid and Mausoleum were tombs; the Statue of Zeus and Temple of Artemis were associated with religious edifices; the Colossus of Rhodes, which represented Helios, the Greek god of the sun, commemorated the heroic resistance of the Rhodians against Demetrius and celebrated their victory; the Hanging Gardens of Babylon and the Lighthouse were utilitarian. Only the Great Pyramid of Giza has survived; all the other wonders were destroyed or fell into ruination centuries ago.

Despite their age, ancient wonders continue to impress and inspire us and over the course of centuries have become models of engineering innovation.

## 484-425 BC:

### List of The Seven Wonders of the Ancient World
by Herodotus giving prominence to the most splendid structures that were worthy of emulation.

| | | | |
|---|---|---|---|
| 1. | Great Pyramid of Giza | 2584-2561 BC | Egypt |
| 2. | Hanging Gardens of Babylon | 605-562 BC | Iraq |
| 3. | Statue of Zeus in Olympia | 466-435 BC | Greece |
| 4. | Temple of Artemis at Ephesus | 550 BC | Turkey |
| 5. | Mausoleum at Halicarnassus | 350 BC | Turkey |
| 6. | Colossus of Rhodes | 292-280 BC | Greece |
| 7. | Lighthouse of Alexandria | 290 BC | Egypt |

For example, the Statue of Liberty in New York is closely related to the Colossus of Rhodes. In its size, gesture of pride and self-confidence and symbolism it was certainly inspired by this ancient wonder. The Rhodian colossus, located in the harbour of the island state of Rhodes, embodied and personified victory in battle and freedom. The Statue of Liberty, located on Liberty Island at the entrance to New York City's harbour, represents freedom, welcome and a safe haven.

Another example of an ancient world wonder that continues to impress us is the Pyramids of Giza. Scientists and archaeologists are still amazed and puzzled by it. The way the construction site was prepared, the scale of the blocks of sandstone and the effort required to stack these heavy, oversized blocks to a height of 146 m is spectacular considering the era in which the pyramids were built and the 'primitive' engineering facilities at the disposal of their engineers. Besides technological inventiveness, the great pyramids were also fundamental to the religious beliefs; they represented the idea of new life that would emerge after death. It seems the pyramids were made to last forever and were meant to represent a powerful eternal life. Ancient Egyptians believed that the pyramid form reflected the afterlife and the layout of the chambers provided the power for spiritual rebirth to occur.

## 1721:

### List of Wonders of the World

by Johann Bernhard Fischer von Erlach, reflecting culture and architectonic value.

| | | | |
|---|---|---|---|
| 1. | Colossus of Rhodes | 292 BC | Greece |
| 2. | Mausoleum at Halicarnassus | 350 BC | Turkey |
| 3. | Mausoleum of Artemis | 550 BC | Turkey |
| 4. | Statue of Zeus at Olympia | 432 BC | Greece |
| 5. | Egyptian pyramids | 2500 BC | Egypt |
| 6. | City of Babylon | 2300 BC | Iraq |
| 7. | Solomon's Temple | 957 BC | Israel |
| 8. | Parthenon | 480 BC | Greece |
| 9. | Temple of Zeus in Athens | 515 BC | Greece |
| 10. | Theatre of Dionysus in Athens | 600 BC | Greece |
| 11. | Temple of Venus at Paphos | 1200 BC | Cyprus |
| 12. | Nineveh Temple | 704 BC | Iraq |
| 13. | Naumachia Domitiani | 1914 BC | Italy |
| 14. | The Mount Athos Colossus | 1655 BC | Macedonia |
| 15. | Cretan Labyrinth at Knossos | 190 BC | Crete |
| 16. | Lighthouse of Alexandria | 285 BC | Egypt |

It seems that this belief and the myth about the afterlife was powerful enough to motivate a workforce of about 100,000 men to construct the building over a period of 23 years.

The 146-m Great Pyramid of Giza, also known as the Pyramid of Khufu, was the tallest building on earth for over 4,300 years, until the Eiffel Tower in Paris surpassed it in 1889. Unlike the Pyramids of Giza, the Eiffel Tower is a remarkably lightweight building for its height. With its minimal structural surface and porosity it provides a more modern example of astounding architectural engineering: it embodies lightness and easily withstands the wind. The structure's rapid construction was facilitated by detailed design planning and off-site prefabrication, which had never been done before. It weighs just 7,300 tonnes and reaches a height of 312 m. The astounding structural and technological achievements aside, the Eiffel Tower makes a strong symbolic gesture to humankind: it aims to bring people together and marks a centre for Paris, France and the whole of Europe. The tower was meant to unite, attract and entertain people from all over the world, and it still does. It currently attracts about 7 million visitors a year, which is half the number of visitors to Disneyland in Tokyo and 2 million more than visit the Colosseum in Rome.

# Modern Wonders

The list of Wonders of the Ancient World has been reinterpreted and enlarged by scholars and travellers over the centuries, and now includes wonders of the Middle Ages and the modern world. Today the lists of world wonders follow classifications such as feats of civil engineering, entire cityscapes and natural sites. Certain commentators have presented lists of wonders that combine these classifications.

The American Society of Civil Engineers (ASCE) aims to celebrate humankind's greatest civil engineering feats of the twentieth century. These achievements demonstrate human technological skill, courage and inspiration, and have had a significant long-term effect on the development of their surroundings and communities. The ASCE selected seven ground-breaking engineering projects from a long list of nominations from various countries around the globe. According to the ASCE, this selection bears testimony to the human spirit and ingenuity of the twentieth century.

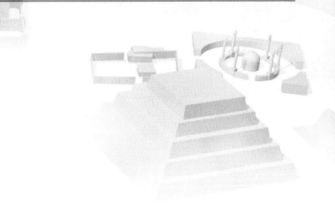

## 1994:

### List of Seven Wonders of the Modern World

by the American Society of Civil Engineers, paying tribute to the twentieth century's greatest civil engineering achievements.

| | | | |
|---|---|---|---|
| 1. | Channel Tunnel | 1987 AD | UK/France |
| 2. | CN Tower | 1973 AD | Canada |
| 3. | Empire State Building | 1930 AD | USA |
| 4. | Golden Gate Bridge | 1933 AD | USA |
| 5. | Itaipu Dam | 1970 AD | Brazil |
| 6. | Zuiderzee Works and the Delta Works | 1950 AD | the Netherlands |
| 7. | Panama Canal | 1880 AD | Panama |

The list of world wonders compiled by the newspaper *USA Today* together with television network ABC News includes the Potala Palace in Tibet, the Old City of Jerusalem, the Polar ice caps, the Papahanaumokuakea Marine National Monument in Hawaii, the Internet, the Mayan ruins and the Great Migration across the Serengeti and Maasai Mara. These are examples of continued human progress in architectural feats (religious or otherwise), excellent engineering, and concern for the future of the planet. This list seems to represent milestones of human technology and spirit, as well as natural phenomena of global importance.

## 2006:

### List of New Wonders of the World

by USA Today and ABC News's Good Morning America, celebrating natural wonders as well as architectural and intellectual feats..

| | | | |
|---|---|---|---|
| 1. | Potala Palace | 600 AD | Lhasa, Tibet |
| 2. | Old City of Jerusalem | 1200 BC | Israel |
| 3. | Polar Ice Caps | | Polar Regions |
| 4. | Papahanaumokuakea Marine National Monument | | Hawaii, USA |
| 5. | Internet | 1983 | Earth |
| 6. | Mayan Ruins | 600 AD | Mexico |
| 7. | Great Serengeti Migration | | Tanzania/Kenya |
| 8. | Grand Canyon | | Arizona, USA |

The list of Seven Wonders of the Industrial World compiled by British author Deborah Cadbury, which the BBC turned into a seven-part documentary series in 2003, represents masterpieces of human technical progress in iron, cement, stone and steel: Bell Rock Lighthouse, iron steamship, Bazalgette's London sewers, the First Transcontinental Railroad, Brooklyn Bridge, the Panama Canal and the Hoover Dam. According to the BBC, each of these masterpieces marked a phase of the Industrial Revolution of the nineteenth and early twentieth centuries and improved people's standard of living.

## 2003:

### List of Seven Wonders of the Industrial World

by Deborah Cadbury and the BBC, based on the greatest feats of human engineering and construction.

| | | | |
|---|---|---|---|
| 1. | Great Eastern steamship, | 1854 AD | England |
| 2. | Brooklyn Bridge, | 1883 AD | USA |
| 3. | Bell Rock Lighthouse | 1807 AD | Scotland |
| 4. | London Sewerage System | 1859 AD | England |
| 5. | Panama Canal, | 1880 AD | Panama |
| 6. | First Transcontinental Railroad | 1863 AD | USA |
| 7. | Hoover Dam | 1931 AD | USA |

World traveller and culinary writer Howard Hillman claims that his list of world wonders is the most comprehensive and best-researched list. He started out with a Top 100 in 1968, but his website now catalogues the world's Top 1,000 travel wonders, including man-made structures as well as natural sites and phenomena. Hillman's list is subject to voting guidelines for an international board of advisors whose members are a mix of all races, sexes, ages and nationalities. The list was also influenced by the many globetrotters whom Hillman has met during his travels, as well as travellers who sent Hillman insightful comments and facts about potential wonders.

Hillman's list aims to represent world wonders without the bias of governmental or political interest, regional or nationalistic opinion, or any other subjective view motivated by unrelated or negative associations. The voter guidelines were intended to guarantee a qualified, impartial list of 1,000 world wonders, but the selection criteria remain unclear. It seems that Hillman compiled a list of must-sees of the world's most marvellous sites, whether natural or cultural, for fellow globetrotters and travellers.

# 1968:

## List of Top 100 Wonders of the World

by Howard Hillman, highlighting the most important and most majestic travel destinations.

| | | | |
|---|---|---|---|
| 1. | Pyramids of Egypt | 2500 BC | Egypt |
| 2. | The Great Wall | 220 BC | China |
| 3. | Taj Mahal | 1630 AD | India |
| 4. | Serengeti Migration | | Kenya / Tanzania |
| 5. | Galapagos Islands | | Ecuador |
| 6. | Grand Canyon | | Arizona, USA |
| 7. | Machu Picchu | 1460 AD | Peru |
| 8. | Iguazú Falls | | Argentina / Brazil |
| 9. | Bali | | Indonesia |
| 10. | Amazon Rain Forest | | Brazil / Peru |
| 11. | Ngorongoro Crater | | Tanzania |
| 12. | Great Barrier Reef | | Australia |
| 13. | Angkor Wat | 12th century AD | Cambodia |
| 14. | Victoria Falls | | Zambia / Zimbabwe |
| 15. | Forbidden City | 1420 AD | Beijing, China |
| 16. | Bagan | 13th century AD | Myanmar |
| 17. | Karnak Temple | 1100 BC | Egypt |
| 18. | Teotihuacan | 2nd century BC | Mexico |
| 19. | Banaue Rice Terraces | 1st century AD | Philippines |
| 20. | Bora Bora | | French Polynesia |
| 21. | Acropolis & its Parthenon | 480 BC | Greece |
| 22. | Potala Palace | 1645 AD | Lhasa, China |
| 23. | Jerusalem Old City | 1004 BC | Israel |
| 24. | Qin Terracotta Warriors | 210 BC | China |
| 25. | Chichén Itzá | 900 AD | Mexico |
| 26. | Petra | 312 BC | Jordan |
| 27. | Nile River Cruise | | Egypt |
| 28. | Easter Island | 1250-1500 AD | Chile |
| 29. | Cappadocia | | Turkey |
| 30. | Colosseum of Rome | 70 AD | Italy |
| 31. | Fjords of Norway | | |
| 32. | St Peter's Basilica | 1626 AD | Vatican City, Italy |
| 33. | Egyptian Museum | 1835 AD | Egypt |
| 34. | Borobudur | 9th century AD | Indonesia |
| 35. | Valley of the Kings | 16th-11th century BC | Egypt |
| 36. | Hong Kong Harbourscape | 221 BC | China |
| 37. | Sistine Chapel | 1421 AD | Vatican City, Italy |
| 38. | Alhambra | 10th century AD | Spain |
| 39. | Louvre Museum | 1973 AD | France |
| 40. | Burj Khalifa | 2010 AD | Dubai, UAE |
| 41. | Canals of Venice, Venice, | 421 AD | Italy |
| 42. | Versailles, | 1682 AD | France |
| 43. | Carlsbad Caverns | | USA |
| 44. | Mecca, | 4th century AD | Arabia |
| 45. | Kathmandu Valley | | Nepal |
| 46. | Metropolitan Museum of Art | 1870 AD | USA |
| 47. | Mount Everest, | | China / Nepal |
| 48. | Antarctic Cruise, | | Multinational |

>>

<<

| | | | |
|---|---|---|---|
| 49. | Temple of the Emerald Buddha | 43 BC | Thailand |
| 50. | Hagia Sofia | 360 AD | Turkey |
| 51. | Pompeii | 79 AD | Italy |
| 52. | Kashmir Valley | | India |
| 53. | Prague Old Town | 800 AD | Czech Republic |
| 54. | Golden Temple | 16th century AD | India |
| 55. | Amalfi Coast & Drive | | Italy |
| 56. | Meenakshi | 13th-6th century AD | India |
| 57. | Chartres Cathedral | 13th century AD | France |
| 58. | Mezquita of Cordoba | 8th century AD | Spain |
| 59. | Damascus Old City / Umayyad | 6300 BC | Syria |
| 60. | Dubrovnik | 7th century AD | Croatia |
| 61. | Uffizi Gallery | 1581 AD | Italy |
| 62. | Rio Panoramic Views | | Brazil |
| 63. | Golden Pavilion | 1397 AD | Japan |
| 64. | Delphi, | 1400 BC | Greece |
| 65. | St Basil's Cathedral | 1561 AD | Russia |
| 66. | Abu Simbel | 1244 BC | Egypt |
| 67. | St Mark's Basilica/Campanile | 1093 AD | Italy |
| 68. | Florence, Cityscape | 16th century | Italy |
| 69. | Kremlin, | 1495 AD | Russia |
| 70. | Varanasi & the Ganges | | India |
| 71. | Li River Cruise China | | |
| 72. | Shwedagon Stupa | 1372 AD | Myanmar |
| 73. | Sahara Desert, | | Multinational |
| 74. | Leaning Tower of Pisa | 1372 AD | Italy |
| 75. | Baalbek | | Lebanon |
| 76. | Mont-St-Michel | 8th century AD | France |
| 77. | Topkapi Palace | 1453 AD | Turkey |
| 78. | Carnival in Rio | 1723 AD | Brazil |
| 79. | Stonehenge | 3000-1500 BC | England |
| 80. | Angel Falls | | Venezuela |
| 81. | Yellowstone | | USA |
| 82. | Santorini | | Greece |
| 83. | Matterhorn | | Switzerland |
| 84. | New York Skyline | 20th century | New York, USA |
| 85. | Marrakesh | 1062 AD | Morocco |
| 86. | Eiffel Tower | 1889 AD | France |
| 87. | Ladakh | | India |
| 88. | Niagara Falls | | Canada / USA |
| 89. | British Museum | 1753 AD | England |
| 90. | Burj Al Arab | 1999 AD | Dubai, UAE |
| 91. | Yangtze River Cruise | | China |
| 92. | Yosemite | | USA |
| 93. | Ayers Rock | | Australia |
| 94. | Hermitage Museum | 1764 AD | Russia |
| 95. | Chambord Chateau | 1547 AD | France |
| 96. | Lijiang / Shangri-La | | China |
| 97. | Neuschwanstein Castle | 19th century | Germany |
| 98. | Banff National Park | | Canada |
| 99. | San Francisco | 1776 AD | USA |
| 100. | Portofino | 986 AD | Italy |

Another example of listing man-made world wonders comes from Bernard Weber, the author who founded the non-profit New7Wonders Foundation. Like others, Weber's aim is to revive the concept of the seven ancient wonders of the world with global campaigns such as the Official New7Wonders of the World, the New7Wonders of Nature and the New7Wonders Cities. With these global campaigns the foundation's aim is to promote cultural diversity by creating events that function as a global platform to bring people from different countries together and where diversity can be exchanged.

## 2007:

### List of New Seven Wonders of the World

by the New7World Wonders Foundation, featuring the most recognizable and representative of humanity's cultural and social history.

| | | | |
|---|---|---|---|
| 1. | Christ the Redeemer | 1931 AD | Brazil |
| 2. | The Great Wall | 220 BC | China |
| 3. | The Pyramid at Chichén Itzá | 8000 BC | Mexico |
| 4. | Taj Mahal | 1630 AD | India |
| 5. | The Roman Colosseum | 70 AD | Italy |
| 6. | Petra | | Jordan |
| 7. | Machu Picchu | | Peru |

A key difference in the compilation of the New7Wonders Foundation's lists is that the wonders are chosen by millions of people from all over the world rather than by one single person. Everyone – children included – can nominate the globe's most awe-inspiring buildings, natural sites or cities by placing their votes. A panel of experts selected 21 finalists from the 77 most popular wonders, these were then whittled down by another round of public voting, resulting in a list of seven world wonders in that particular classification.

The New7Wonders of the World's panel of experts based their votes on the following criteria: structural quality, artistic and cultural value, universal recognisability, and cultural and social diversity. According to the New7Wonders Foundation, the list of wonders of the modern world represents monuments and buildings that are in an acceptable and sufficient state of preservation and in which the creator's vision can be perceived without artificial aids. The new seven wonders of the world according to the New7Wonders Foundation are Chichén Itzá, Christ the Redeemer, the Colosseum, the Great Wall of China, Machu Picchu, Petra and the Taj Mahal.

Criteria such as unique beauty, diversity, ecological significance, historical legacy and even distribution of the nominations over the continents were used for the selection of the seven natural wonders of the world. The New7Wonders of Nature according to the foundation's panel of experts and voters are the Amazon Rainforest in South America, Ha Long Bay in Vietnam, Iguazú Falls in Argentina and Brazil, Jeju Island in South Korea, Indonesia's Komodo Island, the Puerto Princesa Underground River in the Philippines and Table Mountain in South Africa.

## 2011:

### List of New Seven Wonders of Nature

by the New7Wonders Foundation, based on beauty, ecological significance and recognisability.

| | | |
|---|---|---|
| 1. | Iguazú Falls | Argentina/Brazil |
| 2. | Jeju Island | South Korea |
| 3. | Komodo Island | Indonesia |
| 4. | Puerto Princesa Underground River | Philippines |
| 5. | Table Mountain | South Africa |
| 6. | Halong Bay | Vietnam |
| 7. | Amazon Rainforest | spanning Brazil, Peru, Colombia, Venezuela, Ecuador, Bolivia, Guyana, Suriname and French Guiana |

Other commentators, such as the CNN broadcasting company, list natural sites such as Mount Everest in Nepal, the Grand Canyon in the USA, Victoria Falls in Zimbabwe, the Paricutin Volcano in Mexico, the harbour of Rio de Janeiro in Brazil and the phenomenon of the Northern Lights. CNN wanted to publish a list of natural wonders that need to be promoted and protected. Important selection criteria included statistical significance, traditional or historical significance, uniqueness and splendour.

## 2008:

### List of Seven Natural Wonders

by CNN, based on the need for promotion and protection.

| | | |
|---|---|---|
| 1. | Aurora Borealis | northern hemisphere near the North Pole |
| 2. | Harbour of Rio de Janeiro | Brazil |
| 3. | Grand Canyon, Arizona | USA |
| 4. | Great Barrier Reef | Australia |
| 5. | Mount Everest | Nepal |
| 6. | Paricutin | Mexico |
| 7. | Victoria Falls | Zambia |

To some people the Grand Canyon is 'the most beautiful' place to be: 445 km long, between 6 and 30 km wide and over 1.7 km deep. For others 'the most beautiful' place might be on top of Mount Everest at a height of 8.85 km or at the foot of Zuma Rock, a monolith located in Niger state, Nigeria, with a height of 800 m. To others, the spectacle of the glowing sheets and colourful dancing waves called Aurora Borealis (Northern Lights) and Aurora Australis (Southern Lights) near the polar regions ranks as the most beautiful natural phenomenon. The appearance of a rainbow is also often noted for its extraordinary beauty as well as its inexplicability, as are the fury and power of extreme weather features such as destructive hurricanes and tornados, or the beautiful Mammatus clouds that announce heavy storms, a phenomenon whose exact cause remains unknown. Due to their spectacular and violent occurrence, extremely powerful volcano eruptions and earthquakes also inspire a sense of natural beauty, although they embody a destructive threat to humankind and other species.

There are others who claim the Great Barrier Reef is the most beautiful place on earth with its immeasurable biodiversity. The reef extends over 2,600 km and consists of more than 2,900 separate reefs and 900 islands, an area of 344,500 km$^2$ that is the habitat for 400 species of coral, 30 species of whale, dolphin and porpoise, 125 species of shark and stingray, over 1,500 species of fish, 5,000 species of mollusc and much more. The reef is the largest in the world and can easily be seen from outer space.

Whichever natural wonder people consider 'the most beautiful', they become emotional when confronted with them. They fill us with overwhelming feelings, such as love and hate, pleasure and pain, order and chaos, right and wrong, ugliness and beauty – the dichotomies of life. They make us cry, feel grand or small, passionate, proud or stupid. They place people on the precipice of everything and nothing, of power and vulnerability, of attraction and revulsion.

# World Heritage

The United Nations Educational, Scientific and Cultural Organization, or UNESCO, is another author of lists of outstanding sites, whether natural or man-made. In November 1972 UNESCO adopted the World Heritage Convention in order to protect the world's cultural and natural heritage from the increasing threat of damage and destruction. UNESCO distinguishes between cultural, natural and mixed heritage sites, such as monuments, (groups of) buildings and sites of historical, aesthetic, ethnological or anthropological importance. Natural heritage sites include features of aesthetic or scientific importance, geological and physiographical formations, and the habitats of threatened species of animals and plants. Mixed heritage sites are those that combine natural and cultural heritage.

To be included on the UNESCO World Heritage List a site must be of outstanding universal value and meet at least one of the ten selection criteria, of which six represent a cultural value and four a natural value. UNESCO stipulates that a site must meet one or more criteria, the conditions of authenticity and integrity, and the requirement of protection and management to safeguard it.

The UNESCO World Heritage List currently includes 1007 properties – 779 cultural, 197 natural and 31 mixed properties – in 161 countries. According to the UNESCO World Heritage Centre, over 190 countries have ratified the World Heritage Convention.

The United Nations Educational, Scientific and Cultural Organization, or UNESCO, is another author of lists of outstanding sites, whether natural or man-made. In November 1972 UNESCO adopted the World Heritage Convention in order to protect the world's cultural and natural heritage from the increasing threat of damage and destruction. UNESCO distinguishes between cultural, natural and mixed heritage sites, such as monuments, (groups of) buildings and sites of historical, aesthetic, ethnological or anthropological importance. Natural heritage sites include features of aesthetic or scientific importance, geological and physiographical formations, and the habitats of threatened species of animals and plants. Mixed heritage sites are those that combine natural and cultural heritage.

To be included on the UNESCO World Heritage List a site must be of outstanding universal value and meet at least one of the ten selection criteria, of which six represent a cultural value and four a natural value. UNESCO stipulates that a site must meet one or more criteria, the conditions of authenticity and integrity, and the requirement of protection and management to safeguard it.

The UNESCO World Heritage List currently includes 1007 properties – 779 cultural, 197 natural and 31 mixed properties – in 161 countries. According to the UNESCO World Heritage Centre, over 190 countries have ratified the World Heritage Convention.

# 1972 - on going:

## List of World Heritage

by UNESCO, collecting and protecting the global
significant natural and cultural heritage with
universal value. [4]

**Afghanistan**
Minaret and Archaeological Remains of Jam
Cultural Landscape and Archaeological Remains of
the Bamiyan Valley

**Albania**
Butrint
Historic Centres of Berat and Gjirokastra

**Algeria**
Al Qal'a of Beni Hammad
Djémila
M'Zab Valley
Tassili n'Ajjer
Timgad
Tipasa
Kasbah of Algiers

**Andorra**
Madriu-Perafita-Claror Valley

**Argentina**
Los Glaciares National Park
Jesuit Missions of the Guaranis: San Ignacio Mini,
Santa Ana, Nuestra Señora de Loreto and
Santa Maria Mayor (Argentina), Ruins of
Sao Miguel das Missoes (Brazil)
Iguazu National Park
Cueva de las Manos, Rio Pinturas
Peninsula Valdés
Ischigualasto / Talampaya Natural Parks
Jesuit Block and Estancias of Córdoba
Quebrada de Humahuaca
Qhapaq Ñan, Andean Road System

**Armenia**
Monasteries of Haghpat and Sanahin
Cathedral and Churches of Echmiatsin
and the Archaeological Site of Zvartnots
Monastery of Geghard and the Upper Azat Valley

**Australia**
Great Barrier Reef
Kakadu National Park
Willandra Lakes Region
Lord Howe Island Group
Tasmanian Wilderness
Gondwana Rainforests of Australia
Uluru-Kata Tjuta National Park
Wet Tropics of Queensland
Shark Bay, Western Australia
Fraser Island
Australian Fossil Mammal Sites
(Riversleigh / Naracoorte)
Heard and McDonald Islands
Macquarie Island
Greater Blue Mountains Area

Purnululu National Park
Royal Exhibition Building and Carlton Gardens
Sydney Opera House
Australian Convict Sites
Ningaloo Coast

**Austria**
Historic Centre of the City of Salzburg
Palace and Gardens of Schönbrunn
Hallstatt-Dachstein / Salzkammergut
Cultural Landscape
Semmering Railway
City of Graz – Historic Centre and Schloss Eggenberg
Wachau Cultural Landscape
Fertö / Neusiedlersee Cultural Landscape
Historic Centre of Vienna
Prehistoric Pile dwellings around the Alps

**Azerbaijan**
Walled City of Baku with the Shirvanshah's
Palace and Maiden Tower
Gobustan Rock Art Cultural Landscape

**Bahrain**
Qal'at al-Bahrain – Ancient Harbour
and Capital of Dilmun
Pearling, Testimony of an Island Economy

**Bangladesh**
Historic Mosque City of Bagerhat
Ruins of the Buddhist Vihara at Paharpur
The Sundarbans

**Barbados**
Historic Bridgetown and its Garrison

**Belarus**
Białowie a Forest
Mir Castle Complex
Architectural, Residential and Cultural Complex
of the Radziwill Family at Nesvizh
Struve Geodetic Arc

**Belgium**
Flemish Béguinages
La Grand-Place, Brussels
The Four Lifts on the Canal du Centre
and their Environs, La Louvière
and Le Roeulx (Hainaut)
Belfries of Belgium and France
Historic Centre of Brugge
Major Town Houses of
the Architect Victor Horta (Brussels)
Neolithic Flint Mines at Spiennes (Mons)
Notre-Dame Cathedral in Tournai
Plantin-Moretus House-Workshops-Museum Complex
Stoclet House
Major Mining Sites of Wallonia

**Belize**
Belize Barrier Reef Reserve System

**Benin**
Royal Palaces of Abomey

**Bolivia (Plurinational State of)**
City of Potosí
Jesuit Missions of the Chiquitos

Historic City of Sucre
Fuerte de Samaipata
Noel Kempff Mercado National Park
Tiwanaku: Spiritual and Political Centre of
    the Tiwanaku Culture
Qhapaq Ñan, Andean Road System
**Bosnia and Herzegovina**
Old Bridge Area of the Old City of Mostar
Mehmed Paša Sokolovi Bridge in Višegrad
**Botswana**
Tsodilo
Okavango Delta
**Brazil**
Historic Town of Ouro Preto
Historic Centre of the Town of Olinda
Jesuit Missions of the Guaranis: San Ignacio Mini,
    Santa Ana, Nuestra Señora de Loreto and
    Santa Maria Mayor (Argentina), Ruins
    of Sao Miguel das Missoes (Brazil)
Historic Centre of Salvador de Bahia
Sanctuary of Bom Jesus do Congonhas
Iguaçu National Park
Brasilia
Serra da Capivara National Park
Historic Centre of São Luis
Atlantic Forest South-East Reserves
Discovery Coast Atlantic Forest Reserves
Historic Centre of the Town of Diamantina
Central Amazon Conservation Complex
Pantanal Conservation Area
Brazilian Atlantic Islands: Fernando de Noronha
    and Atol das Rocas Reserves
Cerrado Protected Areas: Chapada dos Veadeiros
    and Emas National Parks
Historic Centre of the Town of Goiás
São Francisco Square in the Town of São Cristóvão
Rio de Janeiro: Carioca Landscapes between
    the Mountain and the Sea
**Bulgaria**
Boyana Church
Madara Rider
Rock-Hewn Churches of Ivanovo
Thracian Tomb of Kazanlak
Ancient City of Nessebar
Pirin National Park
Rila Monastery
Srebarna Nature Reserve
Thracian Tomb of Sveshtari
**Burkina Faso**
Ruins of Loropéni
**Cabo Verde**
Cidade Velha, Historic Centre of Ribeira Grande
**Cambodia**
Angkor
Temple of Preah Vihear
**Cameroon**
Dja Faunal Reserve
Sangha Trinational

**Canada**
L'Anse aux Meadows National Historic Site
Nahanni National Park
Dinosaur Provincial Park
Kluane / Wrangell-St. Elias / Glacier Bay /
    Tatshenshini-Alsek
Head-Smashed-In Buffalo Jump
SGang Gwaay
Wood Buffalo National Park
Canadian Rocky Mountain Parks
Historic District of Old Québec
Gros Morne National Park
Old Town Lunenburg
Waterton Glacier International Peace Park
Miguasha National Park
Rideau Canal
Joggins Fossil Cliffs
Landscape of Grand Pré
Red Bay Basque Whaling Station
**Central African Republic**
Manovo-Gounda St Floris National Park
Sangha Trinational
**Chad**
Lakes of Ounianga
**Chile**
Rapa Nui National Park
Churches of Chiloé
Historic Quarter of the Seaport City of Valparaíso
Humberstone and Santa Laura Saltpeter Works
Sewell Mining Town
Qhapaq Ñan, Andean Road System
**China**
Imperial Palaces of the Ming and Qing Dynasties
    in Beijing and Shenyang
Mausoleum of the First Qin Emperor
Mogao Caves
Mount Taishan
Peking Man Site at Zhoukoudian
The Great Wall
Mount Huangshan
Huanglong Scenic and Historic Interest Area
Jiuzhaigou Valley Scenic and Historic Interest Area
Wulingyuan Scenic and Historic Interest Area
Ancient Building Complex in the Wudang Mountains
Historic Ensemble of the Potala Palace, Lhasa
Mountain Resort and its Outlying Temples, Chengde
Temple and Cemetery of Confucius and
    the Kong Family Mansion in Qufu
Lushan National Park
Mount Emei Scenic Area, including
    Leshan Giant Buddha Scenic Area
Ancient City of Ping Yao
Classical Gardens of Suzhou
Old Town of Lijiang
Summer Palace, an Imperial Garden in Beijing
Temple of Heaven: an Imperial Sacrificial Altar in Beijing
Dazu Rock Carvings
Mount Wuyi

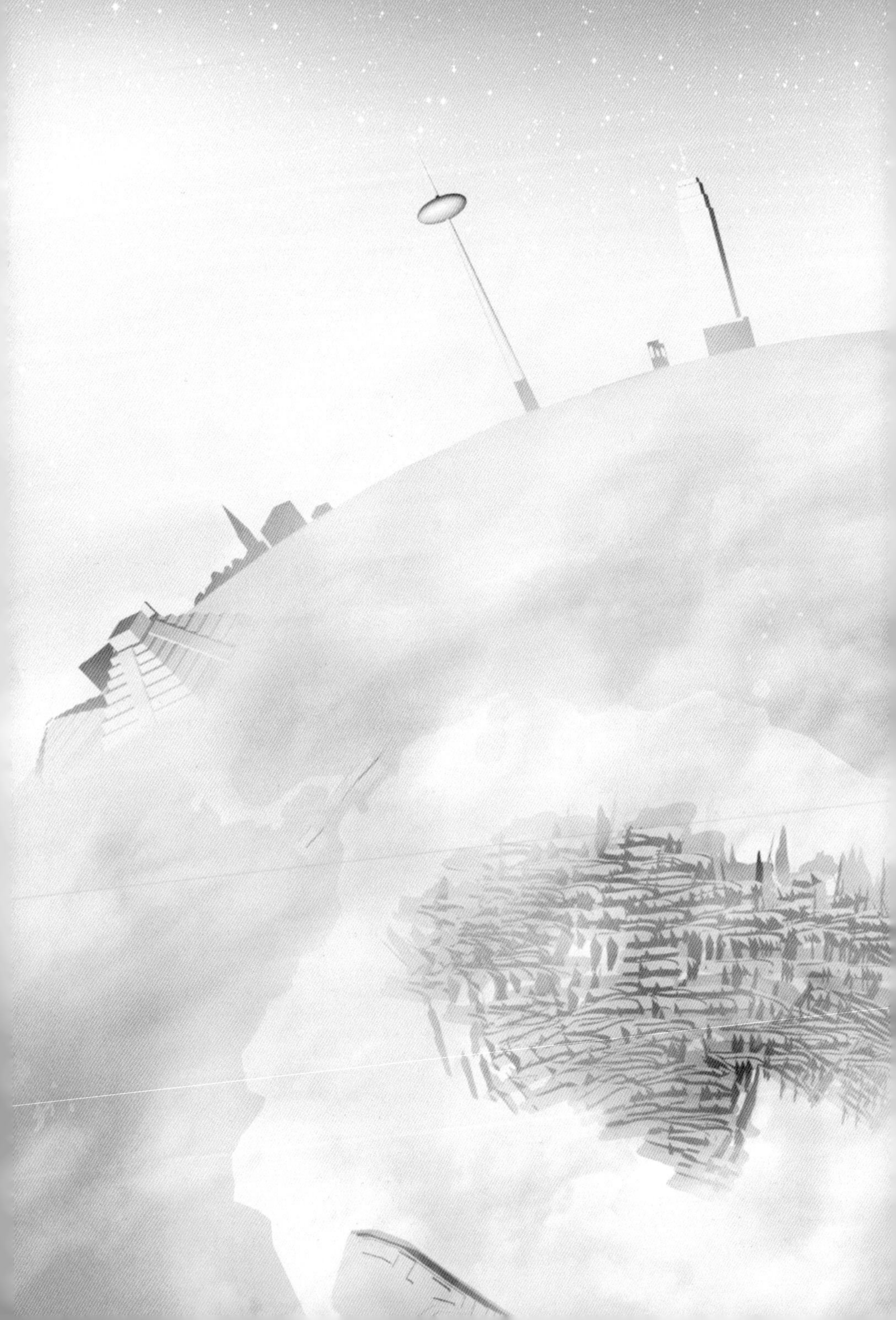

Ancient Villages in Southern Anhui – Xidi and Hongcun
Imperial Tombs of the Ming and Qing Dynasties
Longmen Grottoes
Mount Qingcheng and the Dujiangyan Irrigation System
Yungang Grottoes
Three Parallel Rivers of Yunnan Protected Areas
Capital Cities and Tombs of
   the Ancient Koguryo Kingdom
Historic Centre of Macao
Sichuan Giant Panda Sanctuaries - Wolong,
   Mt Siguniang and Jiajin Mountains
Yin Xu
Kaiping Diaolou and Villages
South China Karst
Fujian Tulou
Mount Sanqingshan National Park
Mount Wutai
China Danxia
Historic Monuments of Dengfeng in
   "The Centre of Heaven and Earth"
West Lake Cultural Landscape of Hangzhou
Chengjiang Fossil Site
Site of Xanadu
Cultural Landscape of Honghe Hani Rice Terraces
Xinjiang Tianshan
Silk Roads: the Routes Network
   of Chang'an-Tianshan Corridor
The Grand Canal

## Colombia
Port, Fortresses and Group of Monuments, Cartagena
Los Katios National Park
Historic Centre of Santa Cruz de Mompox
National Archeological Park of Tierradentro
San Agustin Archaeological Park
Malpelo Fauna and Flora Sanctuary
Coffee Cultural Landscape of Colombia
Qhapaq Ñan, Andean Road System

## Congo
Sangha Trinational

## Costa Rica
Talamanca Range-La Amistad Reserves /
   La Amistad National Park
Cocos Island National Park
Area de Conservación Guanacaste
Precolumbian Chiefdom Settlements
   with Stone Spheres of the Diquís

## Côte d'Ivoire
Mount Nimba Strict Nature Reserve
Taï National Park
Comoé National Park
Historic Town of Grand-Bassam

## Croatia
Historical Complex of Split with the Palace of Diocletian
Old City of Dubrovnik
Plitvice Lakes National Park
Episcopal Complex of the Euphrasian Basilica
   in the Historic Centre of Pore
Historic City of Trogir

The Cathedral of St James in Šibenik
Stari Grad Plain

## Cuba
Old Havana and its Fortification System
Trinidad and the Valley de los Ingenios
San Pedro de la Roca Castle, Santiago de Cuba
Desembarco del Granma National Park
Viñales Valley
Archaeological Landscape of the First
   Coffee Plantations in the South-East of Cuba
Alejandro de Humboldt National Park
Urban Historic Centre of Cienfuegos
Historic Centre of Camagüey

## Cyprus
Paphos
Painted Churches in the Troodos Region
Choirokoitia

## Czech Republic
Historic Centre of Český Krumlov
Historic Centre of Prague
Historic Centre of Telč
Pilgrimage Church of St John of Nepomuk
   at Zelená Hora
Kutná Hora: Historical Town Centre with the Church
   of St Barbara and the Cathedral of Our Lady at Sedlec
Lednice-Valtice Cultural Landscape
Gardens and Castle at Kroměříž
Holašovice Historical Village Reservation
Litomyšl Castle
Holy Trinity Column in Olomouc
Tugendhat Villa in Brno
Jewish Quarter and St Procopius' Basilica in Třebíč

## Democratic People's Republic of Korea
Complex of Koguryo Tombs
Historic Monuments and Sites in Kaesong

## Democratic Republic of the Congo
Virunga National Park
Kahuzi-Biega National Park
Garamba National Park
Salonga National Park
Okapi Wildlife Reserve

## Denmark
Jelling Mounds, Runic Stones and Church
Roskilde Cathedral
Kronborg Castle
Ilulissat Icefjord
Wadden Sea
Stevns Klint

## Dominica
Morne Trois Pitons National Park
Dominican Republic
Colonial City of Santo Domingo

## Ecuador
City of Quito
Galápagos Islands
Sangay National Park
Historic Centre of Santa Ana de los Rios de Cuenca
Qhapaq Ñan, Andean Road System

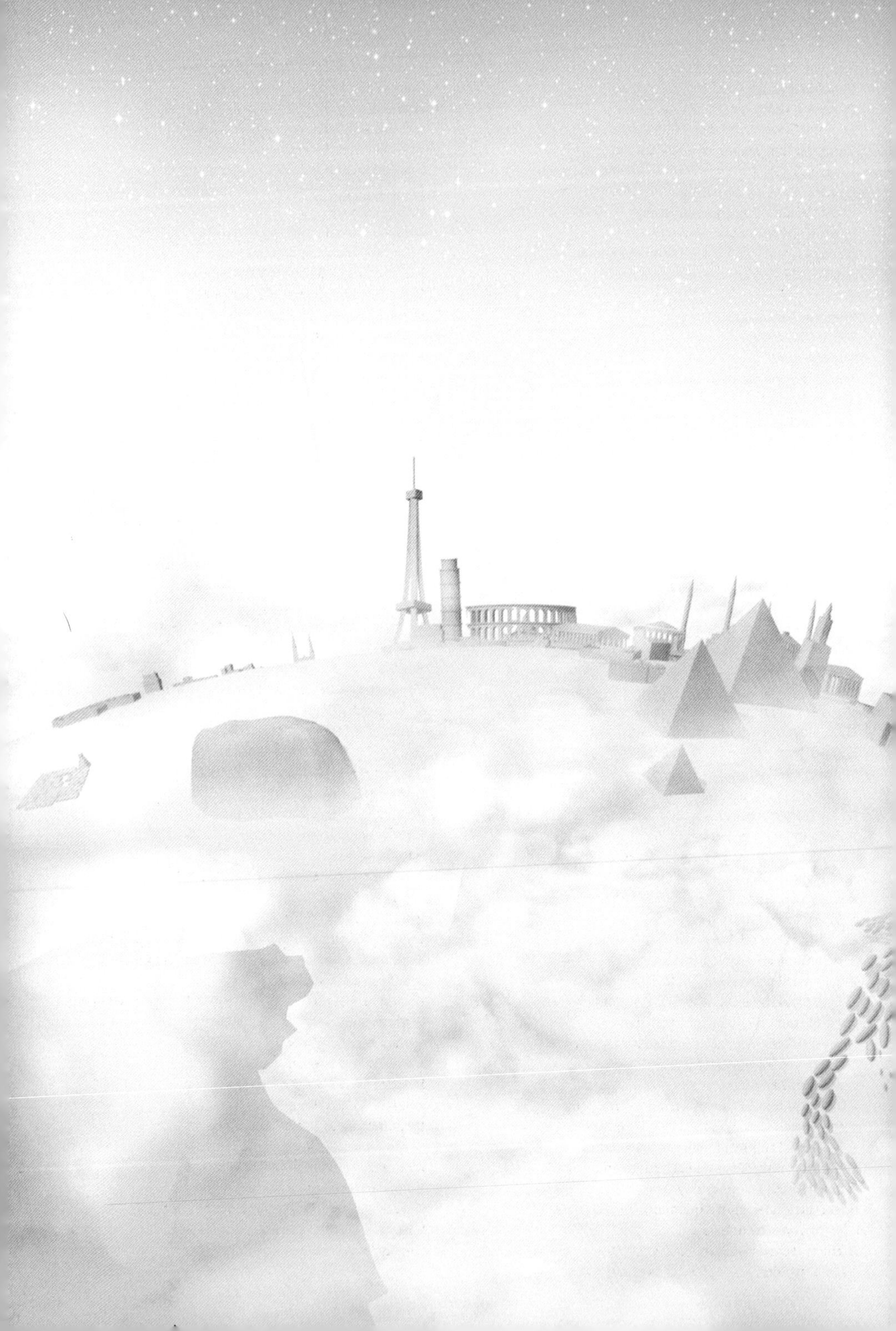

**Egypt**
 Abu Mena
 Ancient Thebes with its Necropolis
 Historic Cairo
 Memphis and its Necropolis – the Pyramid Fields
  from Giza to Dahshur
 Nubian Monuments from Abu Simbel to Philae
 Saint Catherine Area
 Wadi Al-Hitan (Whale Valley)
**El Salvador**
 Joya de Cerén Archaeological Site
**Estonia**
 Historic Centre (Old Town) of Tallinn
 Struve Geodetic Arc
**Ethiopia**
 Simien National Park
 Rock-Hewn Churches, Lalibela
 Fasil Ghebbi, Gondar Region
 Aksum
 Lower Valley of the Awash
 Lower Valley of the Omo
 Tiya
 Harar Jugol, the Fortified Historic Town
 Konso Cultural Landscape
**Fiji**
 Levuka Historical Port Town
**Finland**
 Fortress of Suomenlinna
 Old Rauma
 Petäjävesi Old Church
 Verla Groundwood and Board Mill
 Bronze Age Burial Site of Sammallahdenmäki
 High Coast / Kvarken Archipelago
 Struve Geodetic Arc
**France**
 Chartres Cathedral
 Mont-Saint-Michel and its Bay
 Palace and Park of Versailles
 Prehistoric Sites and Decorated Caves
  of the Vézère Valley
 Vézelay, Church and Hill
 Amiens Cathedral
 Arles, Roman and Romanesque Monuments
 Cistercian Abbey of Fontenay
 Palace and Park of Fontainebleau
 Roman Theatre and its Surroundings and
  the "Triumphal Arch" of Orange
 From the Great Saltworks of Salins-les-Bains to
  the Royal Saltworks of Arc-et-Senans, the Production
  of Open-pan Salt
 Abbey Church of Saint-Savin sur Gartempe
 Gulf of Porto: Calanche of Piana, Gulf of
  Girolata, Scandola Reserve
 Place Stanislas, Place de la Carrière and
  Place d'Alliance in Nancy
 Pont du Gard (Roman Aqueduct)
 Strasbourg – Grande île
 Cathedral of Notre-Dame, Former Abbey
  of Saint-Rémi and Palace of Tau, Reims

 Paris, Banks of the Seine
 Bourges Cathedral
 Historic Centre of Avignon: Papal Palace,
  Episcopal Ensemble and Avignon Bridge
 Canal du Midi
 Historic Fortified City of Carcassonne
 Pyrénées - Mont Perdu
 Historic Site of Lyons
 Routes of Santiago de Compostela in France
 Belfries of Belgium and France
 Jurisdiction of Saint-Emilion
 The Loire Valley between Sully-sur-Loire and Chalonnes
 Provins, Town of Medieval Fairs
 Le Havre, the City Rebuilt by Auguste Perret
 Bordeaux, Port of the Moon
 Fortifications of Vauban
 Lagoons of New Caledonia: Reef Diversity and
  Associated Ecosystems
 Episcopal City of Albi
 Pitons, cirques and remparts of Reunion Island
 Prehistoric Pile dwellings around the Alps
 The Causses and the Cévennes,
  Mediterranean agro-pastoral Cultural Landscape
 Nord-Pas de Calais Mining Basin
 Decorated Cave of Pont d'Arc, known as
  Grotte Chauvet-Pont d'Arc, Ardèche
**Gabon**
 Ecosystem and Relict Cultural Landscape
  of Lopé-Okanda
**Gambia**
 Kunta Kinteh Island and Related Sites
 Stone Circles of Senegambia
**Georgia**
 Bagrati Cathedral and Gelati Monastery
 Historical Monuments of Mtskheta
 Upper Svaneti
**Germany**
 Aachen Cathedral
 Speyer Cathedral
 Würzburg Residence with the Court Gardens
  and Residence Square
 Pilgrimage Church of Wies
 Castles of Augustusburg and Falkenlust at Brühl
 St Mary's Cathedral and St Michael's Church
  at Hildesheim
 Roman Monuments, Cathedral of St Peter and Church
  of Our Lady in Trier
 Frontiers of the Roman Empire
 Hanseatic City of Lübeck
 Palaces and Parks of Potsdam and Berlin
 Abbey and Altenmünster of Lorsch
 Mines of Rammelsberg, Historic Town
  of Goslar and Upper Harz Water Management System
 Maulbronn Monastery Complex
 Town of Bamberg
 Collegiate Church, Castle and Old Town of Quedlinburg
 Völklingen Ironworks
 Messel Pit Fossil Site

Bauhaus and its Sites in Weimar and Dessau
Cologne Cathedral
Luther Memorials in Eisleben and Wittenberg
Classical Weimar
Museumsinsel (Museum Island), Berlin
Wartburg Castle
Garden Kingdom of Dessau-Wörlitz
Monastic Island of Reichenau
Zollverein Coal Mine Industrial Complex in Essen
Historic Centres of Stralsund and Wismar
Upper Middle Rhine Valley
Muskauer Park / Park Mużakowski
Town Hall and Roland on the Marketplace of Bremen
Old town of Regensburg with Stadtamhof
Primeval Beech Forests of the Carpathians
    and the Ancient Beech Forests of Germany
Berlin Modernism Housing Estates
Wadden Sea
Fagus Factory in Alfeld
Prehistoric Pile dwellings around the Alps
Margravial Opera House Bayreuth
Bergpark Wilhelmshöhe
Carolingian Westwork and Civitas Corvey

**Ghana**
Forts and Castles, Volta, Greater Accra, Central
    and Western Regions
Asante Traditional Buildings

**Greece**
Temple of Apollo Epicurius at Bassae
Acropolis, Athens
Archaeological Site of Delphi
Medieval City of Rhodes
Meteora
Mount Athos
Paleochristian and Byzantine Monuments
    of Thessalonika
Sanctuary of Asklepios at Epidaurus
Archaeological Site of Mystras
Archaeological Site of Olympia
Delos
Monasteries of Daphni, Hosios Loukas
    and Nea Moni of Chios
Pythagoreion and Heraion of Samos
Archaeological Site of Aigai (modern name Vergina)
Archaeological Sites of Mycenae and Tiryns
The Historic Centre (Chorá) with the Monastery
    of Saint-John the Theologian and the Cave of
    the Apocalypse on the Island of Pátmos
Old Town of Corfu

**Guatemala**
Antigua Guatemala
Tikal National Park
Archaeological Park and Ruins of Quirigua

**Guinea**
Mount Nimba Strict Nature Reserve

**Haiti**
National History Park – Citadel, Sans Souci, Ramiers

**Holy See**
Historic Centre of Rome, the Properties of
    the Holy See in that City Enjoying Extraterritorial
    Rights and San Paolo Fuori le Mura
Vatican City

**Honduras**
Maya Site of Copan
Rio Plátano Biosphere Reserve

**Hungary**
Budapest, including the Banks of the Danube,
    the Buda Castle Quarter and Andrássy Avenue
Old Village of Hollókő and its Surroundings
Caves of Aggtelek Karst and Slovak Karst
Millenary Benedictine Abbey of Pannonhalma
    and its Natural Environment
Hortobágy National Park - the Puszta
Early Christian Necropolis of Pécs (Sopianae)
Fertö / Neusiedlersee Cultural Landscape
Tokaj Wine Region Historic Cultural Landscape

**Iceland**
Þingvellir National Park
Surtsey

**India**
Agra Fort
Ajanta Caves
Ellora Caves
Taj Mahal
Group of Monuments at Mahabalipuram
Sun Temple, Konârak
Kaziranga National Park
Keoladeo National Park
Manas Wildlife Sanctuary
Churches and Convents of Goa
Fatehpur Sikri
Group of Monuments at Hampi
Khajuraho Group of Monuments
Elephanta Caves
Great Living Chola Temples
Group of Monuments at Pattadakal
Sundarbans National Park
Nanda Devi and Valley of Flowers National Parks
Buddhist Monuments at Sanchi
Humayun's Tomb, Delhi
Qutb Minar and its Monuments, Delhi
Mountain Railways of India
Mahabodhi Temple Complex at Bodh Gaya
Rock Shelters of Bhimbetka
Champaner-Pavagadh Archaeological Park
Chhatrapati Shivaji Terminus
    (formerly Victoria Terminus)
Red Fort Complex
The Jantar Mantar, Jaipur
Western Ghats
Hill Forts of Rajasthan
Great Himalayan National Park Conservation Area
Rani-ki-Vav (the Queen's Stepwell) at Patan, Gujarat

**Indonesia**
Borobudur Temple Compounds

Komodo National Park
Prambanan Temple Compounds
Ujung Kulon National Park
Sangiran Early Man Site
Lorentz National Park
Tropical Rainforest Heritage of Sumatra
Cultural Landscape of Bali Province:
   the Subak System as a Manifestation of
   the Tri Hita Karana Philosophy
**Iran (Islamic Republic of)**
Meidan Emam, Esfahan
Persepolis
Tchogha Zanbil
Takht-e Soleyman
Bam and its Cultural Landscape
Pasargadae
Soltaniyeh
Bisotun
Armenian Monastic Ensembles of Iran
Shushtar Historical Hydraulic System
Sheikh Safi al-din Khānegāh and
   Shrine Ensemble in Ardabil
Tabriz Historic Bazaar Complex
The Persian Garden
Gonbad-e Qābus
Masjed-e Jāmé of Isfahan
Golestan Palace
Shahr-i Sokhta
**Iraq**
Hatra
Ashur (Qal'at Sherqat)
Samarra Archaeological City
Erbil Citadel
**Ireland**
Brú na Bóinne - Archaeological Ensemble of
   the Bend of the Boyne
Sceilg Mhichíl
**Israel**
Masada
Old City of Acre
White City of Tel-Aviv -- the Modern Movement
Biblical Tels - Megiddo, Hazor, Beer Sheba
Incense Route - Desert Cities in the Negev
Bahá'i Holy Places in Haifa and the Western Galilee
Sites of Human Evolution at Mount Carmel:
   The Nahal Me'arot / Wadi el-Mughara Caves
Caves of Maresha and Bet-Guvrin in
   the Judean Lowlands as a Microcosm of
   the Land of the Caves
**Italy**
Rock Drawings in Valcamonica
Church and Dominican Convent of Santa Maria delle
   Grazie with "The Last Supper" by Leonardo da Vinci
Historic Centre of Rome, the Properties of
   the Holy See in that City Enjoying Extraterritorial
   Rights and San Paolo Fuori le Mura
Historic Centre of Florence
Piazza del Duomo, Pisa

Venice and its Lagoon
Historic Centre of San Gimignano
The Sassi and the Park of the Rupestrian Churches
   of Matera
City of Vicenza and the Palladian Villas of the Veneto
Crespi d'Adda
Ferrara, City of the Renaissance, and its Po Delta
Historic Centre of Naples
Historic Centre of Siena
Castel del Monte
Early Christian Monuments of Ravenna
Historic Centre of the City of Pienza
The Trulli of Alberobello
18th-Century Royal Palace at Caserta with
   the Park, the Aqueduct of Vanvitelli, and
   the San Leucio Complex
Archaeological Area of Agrigento
Archaeological Areas of Pompei, Herculaneum
   and Torre Annunziata
Botanical Garden (Orto Botanico), Padua
Cathedral, Torre Civica and Piazza Grande, Modena
Costiera Amalfitana
Portovenere, Cinque Terre, and the Islands
   (Palmaria, Tino and Tinetto)
Residences of the Royal House of Savoy
Su Nuraxi di Barumini
Villa Romana del Casale
Archaeological Area and the Patriarchal Basilica
   of Aquileia
Cilento and Vallo di Diano National Park with
   the Archeological Sites of Paestum and Velia, and
   the Certosa di Padula
Historic Centre of Urbino
Villa Adriana (Tivoli)
Assisi, the Basilica of San Francesco and
   Other Franciscan Sites
City of Verona
Isole Eolie (Aeolian Islands)
Villa d'Este, Tivoli
Late Baroque Towns of the Val di Noto
   (South-Eastern Sicily)
Sacri Monti di Piedmont and Lombardy
Monte San Giorgio
Etruscan Necropolises of Cerveteri and Tarquinia
Val d'Orcia
Syracuse and the Rocky Necropolis of Pantalica
Genoa: Le Strade Nuove and the system of
   the Palazzi dei Rolli
Mantua and Sabbioneta
Rhaetian Railway in the Albula / Bernina Landscapes
The Dolomites
Longobards in Italy. Places of the Power (568-774 A.D.)
Prehistoric Pile dwellings around the Alps
Medici Villas and Gardens in Tuscany
Mount Etna
Vineyard Landscape of Piedmont: Langhe-Roero
   and Monferrato

## Japan
Buddhist Monuments in the Horyu-ji Area
Himeji-jo
Shirakami-Sanchi
Yakushima
Historic Monuments of Ancient Kyoto
  (Kyoto, Uji and Otsu Cities)
Historic Villages of Shirakawa-go and Gokayama
Hiroshima Peace Memorial (Genbaku Dome)
Itsukushima Shinto Shrine
Historic Monuments of Ancient Nara
Shrines and Temples of Nikko
Gusuku Sites and Related Properties of
  the Kingdom of Ryukyu
Sacred Sites and Pilgrimage Routes in
  the Kii Mountain Range
Shiretoko
Iwami Ginzan Silver Mine and its Cultural Landscape
Hiraizumi – Temples, Gardens and Archaeological
  Sites Representing the Buddhist Pure Land
Ogasawara Islands
Fujisan, sacred place and source of artistic inspiration
Tomioka Silk Mill and Related Sites

## Jerusalem (Site proposed by Jordan)
Old City of Jerusalem and its Walls

## Jordan
Petra
Quseir Amra
Um er-Rasas (Kastrom Mefa'a)
Wadi Rum Protected Area

## Kazakhstan
Mausoleum of Khoja Ahmed Yasawi
Petroglyphs within the Archaeological
  Landscape of Tamgaly
Saryarka – Steppe and Lakes of Northern Kazakhstan
Silk Roads: the Routes Network
  of Chang'an-Tianshan Corridor

## Kenya
Lake Turkana National Parks
Mount Kenya National Park/Natural Forest
Lamu Old Town
Sacred Mijikenda Kaya Forests
Fort Jesus, Mombasa
Kenya Lake System in the Great Rift Valley

## Kiribati
Phoenix Islands Protected Area

## Kyrgyzstan
Sulaiman-Too Sacred Mountain
Silk Roads: the Routes Network
  of Chang'an-Tianshan Corridor

## Lao People's Democratic Republic
Town of Luang Prabang
Vat Phou and Associated Ancient Settlements
  within the Champasak Cultural Landscape

## Latvia
Historic Centre of Riga
Struve Geodetic Arc

## Lebanon
Anjar
Baalbek
Byblos
Tyre
Ouadi Qadisha (the Holy Valley) and the Forest of
  the Cedars of God (Horsh Arz el-Rab)

## Lesotho
Maloti-Drakensberg Park

## Libya
Archaeological Site of Cyrene
Archaeological Site of Leptis Magna
Archaeological Site of Sabratha
Rock-Art Sites of Tadrart Acacus
Old Town of Ghadamès

## Lithuania
Vilnius Historic Centre
Curonian Spit
Kernavė Archaeological Site (Cultural
  Reserve of Kernavè)
Struve Geodetic Arc

## Luxembourg
City of Luxembourg: its Old Quarters and Fortifications

## Madagascar
Tsingy de Bemaraha Strict Nature Reserve
Royal Hill of Ambohimanga
Rainforests of the Atsinanana

## Malawi
Lake Malawi National Park
Chongoni Rock-Art Area

## Malaysia
Gunung Mulu National Park
Kinabalu Park
Melaka and George Town, Historic Cities of
  the Straits of Malacca
Archaeological Heritage of the Lenggong Valley

## Mali
Timbuktu
Old Towns of Djenné
Cliff of Bandiagara (Land of the Dogons)
Tomb of Askia

## Malta
City of Valletta
Megalithic Temples of Malta
Ħal Saflieni Hypogeum

## Marshall Islands
Bikini Atoll Nuclear Test Site

## Mauritania
Banc d'Arguin National Park
Ancient Ksour of Ouadane, Chinguetti, Tichitt
  and Oualata

## Mauritius
Aapravasi Ghat
Le Morne Cultural Landscape

## Mexico
Historic Centre of Mexico City and Xochimilco
Historic Centre of Oaxaca and Archaeological
  Site of Monte Albán

Historic Centre of Puebla
Pre-Hispanic City and National Park of Palenque
Pre-Hispanic City of Teotihuacan
Sian Ka'an
Historic Town of Guanajuato and Adjacent Mines
Pre-Hispanic City of Chichen-Itza
Historic Centre of Morelia
El Tajin, Pre-Hispanic City
Historic Centre of Zacatecas
Rock Paintings of the Sierra de San Francisco
Whale Sanctuary of El Vizcaino
Earliest 16th-Century Monasteries on
    the Slopes of Popocatepetl
Historic Monuments Zone of Querétaro
Pre-Hispanic Town of Uxmal
Hospicio Cabañas, Guadalajara
Archaeological Zone of Paquimé, Casas Grandes
Historic Monuments Zone of Tlacotalpan
Archaeological Monuments Zone of Xochicalco
Historic Fortified Town of Campeche
Ancient Maya City and Protected Tropical Forests
    of Calakmul, Campeche
Franciscan Missions in the Sierra Gorda of Querétaro
Luis Barragán House and Studio
Islands and Protected Areas of the Gulf of California
Agave Landscape and Ancient Industrial Facilities
    of Tequila
Central University City Campus of the
    Universidad Nacional Autónoma de México (UNAM)
Monarch Butterfly Biosphere Reserve
Protective town of San Miguel and the Sanctuary
    of Jesús Nazareno de Atotonilco
Camino Real de Tierra Adentro
Prehistoric Caves of Yagul and Mitla in
    the Central Valley of Oaxaca
El Pinacate and Gran Desierto de Altar
    Biosphere Reserve

**Moldova, Republic of**
Struve Geodetic Arc

**Mongolia**
Uvs Nuur Basin
Orkhon Valley Cultural Landscape
Petroglyphic Complexes of the Mongolian Altai

**Montenegro**
Natural and Culturo-Historical Region of Kotor
Durmitor National Park

**Morocco**
Medina of Fez
Medina of Marrakesh
Ksar of Ait-Ben-Haddou
Historic City of Meknes
Archaeological Site of Volubilis
Medina of Tétouan (formerly known as Titawin)
Medina of Essaouira (formerly Mogador)
Portuguese City of Mazagan (El Jadida)
Rabat, Modern Capital and Historic City:
    a Shared Heritage

**Mozambique**
Island of Mozambique

**Myanmar**
Pyu Ancient Cities

**Namibia**
Twyfelfontein or /Ui-//aes
Namib Sand Sea

**Nepal**
Kathmandu Valley
Sagarmatha National Park
Chitwan National Park
Lumbini, the Birthplace of the Lord Buddha

**Netherlands**
Schokland and Surroundings
Defence Line of Amsterdam
Historic Area of Willemstad, Inner City
    and Harbour, Curaçao
Mill Network at Kinderdijk-Elshout
Ir.D.F. Woudagemaal (D.F. Wouda Steam
    Pumping Station)
Droogmakerij de Beemster (Beemster Polder)
Rietveld Schröderhuis (Rietveld Schröder House)
Wadden Sea
Seventeenth-Century Canal Ring Area of
    Amsterdam inside the Singelgracht
Van Nellefabriek

**New Zealand**
Te Wahipounamu – South West New Zealand
Tongariro National Park
New Zealand Sub-Antarctic Islands

**Nicaragua**
Ruins of León Viejo
León Cathedral

**Niger**
Air and Ténéré Natural Reserves
W National Park of Niger
Historic Centre of Agadez

**Nigeria**
Sukur Cultural Landscape
Osun-Osogbo Sacred Grove

**Norway**
Bryggen
Urnes Stave Church
Røros Mining Town and the Circumference
Rock Art of Alta
Vegaøyan -- The Vega Archipelago
Struve Geodetic Arc
West Norwegian Fjords – Geirangerfjord
    and Nærøyfjord

**Oman**
Bahla Fort
Archaeological Sites of Bat, Al-Khutm and Al-Ayn
Land of Frankincense
Aflaj Irrigation Systems of Oman

**Pakistan**
Archaeological Ruins at Moenjodaro
Buddhist Ruins of Takht-i-Bahi and Neighbouring
    City Remains at Sahr-i-Bahlol

Taxila
Fort and Shalamar Gardens in Lahore
Historical Monuments at Makli, Thatta
Rohtas Fort

**Palau**
Rock Islands Southern Lagoon

**Palestine**
Birthplace of Jesus: Church of the Nativity and
the Pilgrimage Route, Bethlehem
Palestine: Land of Olives and Vines –
Cultural Landscape of Southern Jerusalem, Battir

**Panama**
Fortifications on the Caribbean Side of Panama:
Portobelo-San Lorenzo
Darien National Park
Talamanca Range-La Amistad Reserves /
La Amistad National Park
Archaeological Site of Panamá Viejo and
Historic District of Panamá
Coiba National Park and its Special Zone
of Marine Protection

**Papua New Guinea**
Kuk Early Agricultural Site

**Paraguay**
Jesuit Missions of La Santisima Trinidad de Paraná
and Jesús de Tavarangue

**Peru**
City of Cuzco
Historic Sanctuary of Machu Picchu
Chavin (Archaeological Site)
Huascarán National Park
Chan Chan Archaeological Zone
Manú National Park
Historic Centre of Lima
Rio Abiseo National Park
Lines and Geoglyphs of Nasca and Pampas de Jumana
Historical Centre of the City of Arequipa
Sacred City of Caral-Supe
Qhapaq Ñan, Andean Road System

**Philippines**
Baroque Churches of the Philippines
Tubbataha Reefs Natural Park
Rice Terraces of the Philippine Cordilleras
Historic Town of Vigan
Puerto-Princesa Subterranean River National Park
Mount Hamiguitan Range Wildlife Sanctuary

**Poland**
Historic Centre of Kraków
Wieliczka and Bochnia Royal Salt Mines
Auschwitz Birkenau German Nazi Concentration
and Extermination Camp (1940-1945)
Białowieża Forest
Historic Centre of Warsaw
Old City of Zamość
Castle of the Teutonic Order in Malbork
Medieval Town of Toruń
Kalwaria Zebrzydowska: the Mannerist
Architectural and Park Landscape Complex
and Pilgrimage Park

Churches of Peace in Jawor and Świdnica
Wooden Churches of Southern Małopolska
Muskauer Park / Park Mużakowski
Centennial Hall in Wrocław
Wooden Tserkvas of the Carpathian Region
in Poland and Ukraine

**Portugal**
Central Zone of the Town of Angra do Heroismo in
the Azores
Convent of Christ in Tomar
Monastery of Batalha
Monastery of the Hieronymites and Tower of
Belém in Lisbon
Historic Centre of Évora
Monastery of Alcobaça
Cultural Landscape of Sintra
Historic Centre of Oporto
Prehistoric Rock Art Sites in the Côa Valley
and Siega Verde
Laurisilva of Madeira
Alto Douro Wine Region
Historic Centre of Guimarães
Landscape of the Pico Island Vineyard Culture
Garrison Border Town of Elvas and its Fortifications
University of Coimbra – Alta and Sofia

**Qatar**
Al Zubarah Archaeological Site

**Republic of Korea**
Haeinsa Temple Janggyeong Panjeon, the
Depositories for the Tripitaka Koreana Woodblocks
Jongmyo Shrine
Seokguram Grotto and Bulguksa Temple
Changdeokgung Palace Complex
Hwaseong Fortress
Gochang, Hwasun and Ganghwa Dolmen Sites
Gyeongju Historic Areas
Jeju Volcanic Island and Lava Tubes
Royal Tombs of the Joseon Dynasty
Historic Villages of Korea: Hahoe and Yangdong
Namhansanseong

**Romania**
Danube Delta
Churches of Moldavia
Monastery of Horezu
Villages with Fortified Churches in Transylvania
Dacian Fortresses of the Orastie Mountains
Historic Centre of Sighişoara
Wooden Churches of Maramureş

**Russian Federation**
Historic Centre of Saint Petersburg and
Related Groups of Monuments
Kizhi Pogost
Kremlin and Red Square, Moscow
Cultural and Historic Ensemble of the Solovetsky Islands
Historic Monuments of Novgorod and Surroundings
White Monuments of Vladimir and Suzdal
Architectural Ensemble of the Trinity Sergius Lavra
in Sergiev Posad

Church of the Ascension, Kolomenskoye
Virgin Komi Forests
Lake Baikal
Volcanoes of Kamchatka
Golden Mountains of Altai
Western Caucasus
Curonian Spit
Ensemble of the Ferapontov Monastery
Historic and Architectural Complex of
  the Kazan Kremlin
Central Sikhote-Alin
Citadel, Ancient City and Fortress Buildings
  of Derbent
Uvs Nuur Basin
Ensemble of the Novodevichy Convent
Natural System of Wrangel Island Reserve
Historical Centre of the City of Yaroslavl
Struve Geodetic Arc
Putorana Plateau
Lena Pillars Nature Park
Bolgar Historical and Archaeological Complex

**Saint Kitts and Nevis**
Brimstone Hill Fortress National Park

**Saint Lucia**
Pitons Management Area

**San Marino**
San Marino Historic Centre and Mount Titano

**Saudi Arabia**
Al-Hijr Archaeological Site (Madâin Sâlih)
At-Turaif District in ad-Dir'iyah
Historic Jeddah, the Gate to Makkah

**Senegal**
Island of Gorée
Niokolo-Koba National Park
Djoudj National Bird Sanctuary
Island of Saint-Louis
Stone Circles of Senegambia
Saloum Delta
Bassari Country: Bassari, Fula
  and Bedik Cultural Landscapes

**Serbia**
Stari Ras and Sopoćani
Studenica Monastery
Medieval Monuments in Kosovo
Gamzigrad-Romuliana, Palace of Galerius

**Seychelles**
Aldabra Atoll
Vallée de Mai Nature Reserve

**Slovakia**
Historic Town of Banská Štiavnica and
  the Technical Monuments in its Vicinity
Levoča, Spišský Hrad and the Associated
  Cultural Monuments
Vlkolínec
Caves of Aggtelek Karst and Slovak Karst
Bardejov Town Conservation Reserve
Primeval Beech Forests of the Carpathians and
  the Ancient Beech Forests of Germany

Wooden Churches of the Slovak part of
  the Carpathian Mountain Area
**Slovenia**
Škocjan Caves
Prehistoric Pile dwellings around the Alps
Heritage of Mercury. Almadén and Idrija
**Solomon Islands**
East Rennell
**South Africa**
Fossil Hominid Sites of South Africa
iSimangaliso Wetland Park
Robben Island
Maloti-Drakensberg Park
Mapungubwe Cultural Landscape
Cape Floral Region Protected Areas
Vredefort Dome
Richtersveld Cultural and Botanical Landscape
**Spain**
Alhambra, Generalife and Albayzin, Granada
Burgos Cathedral
Historic Centre of Cordoba
Monastery and Site of the Escurial, Madrid
Works of Antoni Gaudí
Cave of Altamira and Paleolithic Cave Art
  of Northern Spain
Monuments of Oviedo and the Kingdom of the Asturias
Old Town of Ávila with its Extra-Muros Churches
Old Town of Segovia and its Aqueduct
Santiago de Compostela (Old Town)
Garajonay National Park
Historic City of Toledo
Mudejar Architecture of Aragon
Old Town of Cáceres
Cathedral, Alcázar and Archivo de Indias in Seville
Old City of Salamanca
Poblet Monastery
Archaeological Ensemble of Mérida
Route of Santiago de Compostela
Royal Monastery of Santa María de Guadalupe
Doñana National Park
Historic Walled Town of Cuenca
La Lonja de la Seda de Valencia
Las Médulas
Palau de la Música Catalana and
  Hospital de Sant Pau, Barcelona
Pyrénées - Mont Perdu
San Millán Yuso and Suso Monasteries
Prehistoric Rock Art Sites in the Côa Valley
  and Siega Verde
Rock Art of the Mediterranean Basin on
  the Iberian Peninsula
University and Historic Precinct of Alcalá de Henares
Ibiza, Biodiversity and Culture
San Cristóbal de La Laguna
Archaeological Ensemble of Tárraco
Archaeological Site of Atapuerca
Catalan Romanesque Churches of the Vall de Boí
Palmeral of Elche

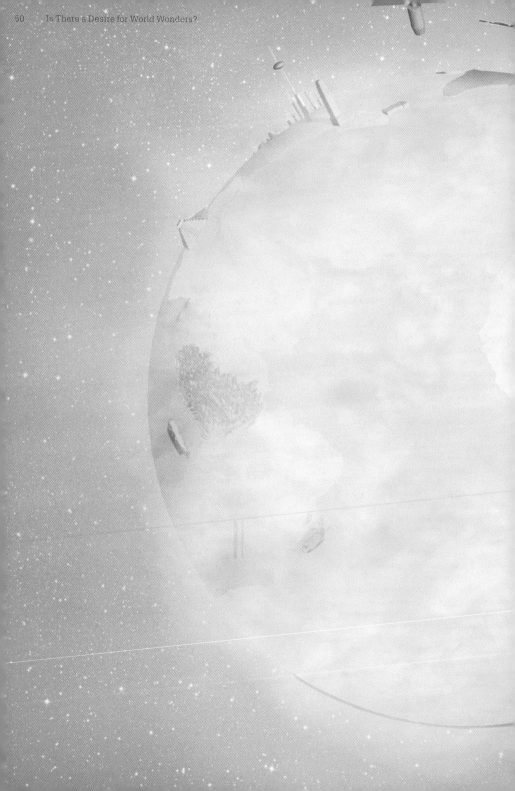

Roman Walls of Lugo
Aranjuez Cultural Landscape
Renaissance Monumental Ensembles
    of Úbeda and Baeza
Vizcaya Bridge
Teide National Park
Tower of Hercules
Cultural Landscape of the Serra de Tramuntana
Heritage of Mercury. Almadén and Idrija

**Sri Lanka**
Ancient City of Polonnaruwa
Ancient City of Sigiriya
Sacred City of Anuradhapura
Old Town of Galle and its Fortifications
Sacred City of Kandy
Sinharaja Forest Reserve
Golden Temple of Dambulla
Central Highlands of Sri Lanka

**Sudan**
Gebel Barkal and the Sites of the Napatan Region
Archaeological Sites of the Island of Meroe

**Suriname**
Central Suriname Nature Reserve
Historic Inner City of Paramaribo

**Sweden**
Royal Domain of Drottningholm
Birka and Hovgården
Engelsberg Ironworks
Rock Carvings in Tanum
Skogskyrkogården
Hanseatic Town of Visby
Church Town of Gammelstad, Luleå
Laponian Area
Naval Port of Karlskrona
Agricultural Landscape of Southern Öland
High Coast / Kvarken Archipelago
Mining Area of the Great Copper Mountain in Falun
Grimeton Radio Station, Varberg
Struve Geodetic Arc
Decorated Farmhouses of Hälsingland

**Switzerland**
Abbey of St Gall
Benedictine Convent of St John at Müstair
Old City of Berne
Three Castles, Defensive Wall and Ramparts of
    the Market-Town of Bellinzona
Swiss Alps Jungfrau-Aletsch
Monte San Giorgio
Lavaux, Vineyard Terraces
Rhaetian Railway in the Albula / Bernina Landscapes
Swiss Tectonic Arena Sardona
La Chaux-de-Fonds / Le Locle,
    Watchmaking Town Planning
Prehistoric Pile dwellings around the Alps

**Syrian Arab Republic**
Ancient City of Damascus
Ancient City of Bosra
Site of Palmyra

Ancient City of Aleppo
Crac des Chevaliers and Qal'at Salah El-Din
Ancient Villages of Northern Syria

**Tajikistan**
Proto-urban Site of Sarazm
Tajik National Park (Mountains of the Pamirs)

**Tanzania, United Republic of**
Ngorongoro Conservation Area
Ruins of Kilwa Kisiwani and Ruins of Songo Mnara
Serengeti National Park
Selous Game Reserve
Kilimanjaro National Park
Stone Town of Zanzibar
Kondoa Rock-Art Sites

**Thailand**
Historic City of Ayutthaya
Historic Town of Sukhothai and
    Associated Historic Towns
Thungyai-Huai Kha Khaeng Wildlife Sanctuaries
Ban Chiang Archaeological Site
Dong Phayayen-Khao Yai Forest Complex

**the Former Yugoslav Republic of Macedonia**
Natural and Cultural Heritage of the Ohrid region

**Togo**
Koutammakou, the Land of the Batammariba

**Tunisia**
Amphitheatre of El Jem
Archaeological Site of Carthage
Medina of Tunis
Ichkeul National Park
Punic Town of Kerkuane and its Necropolis
Kairouan
Medina of Sousse
Dougga / Thugga

**Turkey**
Göreme National Park and the Rock Sites of Cappadocia
Great Mosque and Hospital of Divriği
Historic Areas of Istanbul
Hattusha: the Hittite Capital
Nemrut Dağ
Hierapolis-Pamukkale
Xanthos-Letoon
City of Safranbolu
Archaeological Site of Troy
Selimiye Mosque and its Social Complex
Neolithic Site of Çatalhöyük
Bursa and Cumalıkızık: the Birth of the Ottoman Empire
Pergamon and its Multi-Layered Cultural Landscape

**Turkmenistan**
State Historical and Cultural Park "Ancient Merv"
Kunya-Urgench
Parthian Fortresses of Nisa

**Uganda**
Bwindi Impenetrable National Park
Rwenzori Mountains National Park
Tombs of Buganda Kings at Kasubi

**Ukraine**
Kiev: Saint-Sophia Cathedral and Related
    Monastic Buildings, Kiev-Pechersk Lavra

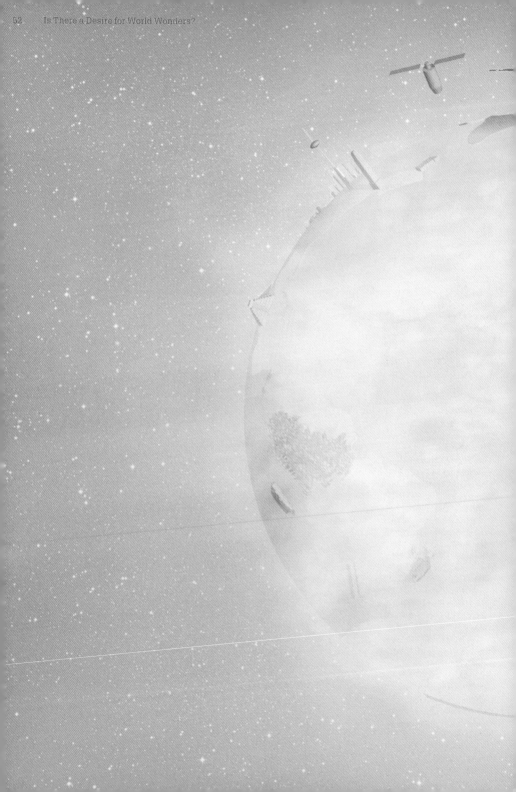

L'viv – the Ensemble of the Historic Centre
Struve Geodetic Arc
Primeval Beech Forests of the Carpathians and
    the Ancient Beech Forests of Germany
Residence of Bukovinian and Dalmatian Metropolitans
Ancient City of Tauric Chersonese and its Chora
Wooden Tserkvas of the Carpathian Region
    in Poland and Ukraine

**United Arab Emirates**
    Cultural Sites of Al Ain (Hafit, Hili, Bidaa Bint Saud
      and Oases Areas)

**United Kingdom of Great Britain
and Northern Ireland**
    Castles and Town Walls of King Edward in Gwynedd
    Durham Castle and Cathedral
    Giant's Causeway and Causeway Coast
    Ironbridge Gorge
    St Kilda
    Stonehenge, Avebury and Associated Sites
    Studley Royal Park including the Ruins of
      Fountains Abbey
    Blenheim Palace
    City of Bath
    Frontiers of the Roman Empire
    Palace of Westminster and Westminster Abbey
      including Saint Margaret's Church
    Canterbury Cathedral, St Augustine's Abbey,
      and St Martin's Church
    Henderson Island
    Tower of London
    Gough and Inaccessible Islands
    Old and New Towns of Edinburgh
    Maritime Greenwich
    Heart of Neolithic Orkney
    Blaenavon Industrial Landscape
    Historic Town of St George and
      Related Fortifications, Bermuda
    Derwent Valley Mills
    Dorset and East Devon Coast
    New Lanark
    Saltaire
    Royal Botanic Gardens, Kew
    Liverpool – Maritime Mercantile City
    Cornwall and West Devon Mining Landscape
    Pontcysyllte Aqueduct and Canal

**United States of America**
    Mesa Verde National Park
    Yellowstone National Park
    Everglades National Park
    Grand Canyon National Park
    Independence Hall
    Kluane / Wrangell-St. Elias / Glacier Bay /
      Tatshenshini-Alsek
    Redwood National and State Parks
    Mammoth Cave National Park
    Olympic National Park
    Cahokia Mounds State Historic Site
    Great Smoky Mountains National Park
    La Fortaleza and San Juan National Historic Site
      in Puerto Rico

Statue of Liberty
Yosemite National Park
Chaco Culture
Hawaii Volcanoes National Park
Monticello and the University of Virginia
    in Charlottesville
Taos Pueblo
Carlsbad Caverns National Park
Waterton Glacier International Peace Park
Papahānaumokuākea
Monumental Earthworks of Poverty Point

**Uruguay**
    Historic Quarter of the City of Colonia del Sacramento

**Uzbekistan**
    Itchan Kala
    Historic Centre of Bukhara
    Historic Centre of Shakhrisyabz
    Samarkand – Crossroad of Cultures

**Vanuatu**
    Chief Roi Mata's Domain

**Venezuela (Bolivarian Republic of)**
    Coro and its Port
    Canaima National Park
    Ciudad Universitaria de Caracas

**Viet Nam**
    Complex of Hué Monuments
    Ha Long Bay
    Hoi An Ancient Town
    My Son Sanctuary
    Phong Nha-Ke Bang National Park
    Central Sector of the Imperial Citadel of
      Thang Long - Hanoi
    Citadel of the Ho Dynasty
    Trang An Landscape Complex

**Yemen**
    Old Walled City of Shibam
    Old City of Sana'a
    Historic Town of Zabid
    Socotra Archipelago

**Zambia**
    Mosi-oa-Tunya / Victoria Falls

**Zimbabwe**
    Mana Pools National Park, Sapi and
      Chewore Safari Areas
    Great Zimbabwe National Monument
    Khami Ruins National Monument
    Mosi-oa-Tunya / Victoria Falls
    Matobo Hills

# Cataloguing the Creative Spirit.
## Conclusion

'The more clearly we can focus
our attention on the wonders and realities of the universe
about us the less taste we shall have for destruction.
Wonder and humility are wholesome emotions, and they
do not exist side by side with a lust for destruction.'

Rachel Carson (American biologist and conservationist, 1907-1964)

However diverse these inventories may be, their authors share one thing in common: they want to collect and record the wonderful and precious creations of this world. Collectively these inventories form a history of a creative spirit, each of them illustrating something extraordinary on a universal scale.
They represent a catalogue of contemporary testimonies to human creativity and natural conditions. None of the authors have ranked their selections, so the sites and phenomena are of equal merit. They describe their selections as unique, beautiful, spectacular, rich, spiritual, intellectual, artistic, superlative

or inventive. Whether driven by love, fear, death, hope, belief, tradition, symbolic meaning, responsibility or science, all these listed wonders inspire awe and amazement. It is our duty to take stock of these lists of wonders and continue to add to them.

But why? Because these sites make people think, not once, but time and time again. They impress us, intrigue us, and bring the world around them to a momentary standstill, capturing us in wonderment. They inspire admiration, question any form of limitation, challenge and evoke the power of creative processes, whether natural or technological. They drive us to embrace our fears, dreams and fantasies to confront the enigmas of space and time. They keep alive the spirit of the mysterious, universal beauty and wonderment. Altogether these selected sites exemplify the continued progress that people have made throughout history as well as their concern for the future of Planet Earth.

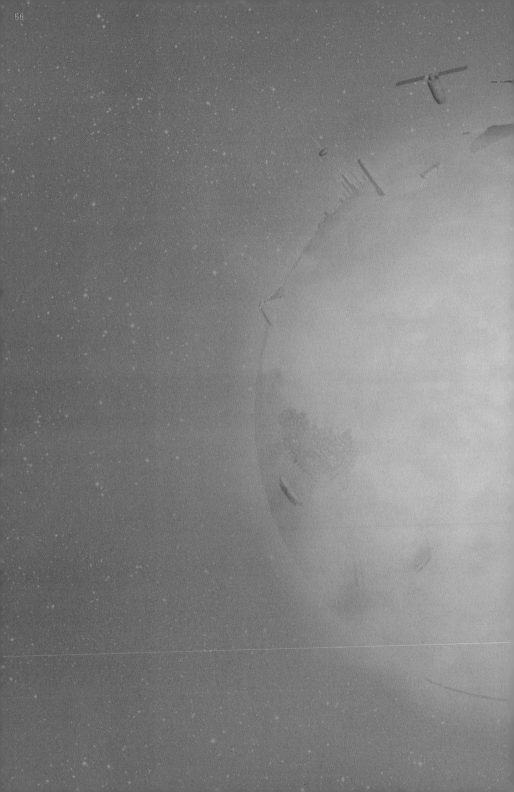

# What Makes a Man-Made Wonder?

Tihamér Salij

# Mystery. The Act of Wondering

*'When the first encounter with some object surprises us, and we judge it to be new, or very different from what we knew in the past or what we supposed it was going to be, this makes us wonder and be astonished at it.'*

René Descartes (French philosopher, 1596-1650)

In general, the word 'wonder' is used in a rich variety of contexts. We experience wonder when we discover how something works and happens, when we see something for the first time or when something occurs repeatedly. Something we absorb through our senses, visual, tactile or as smell could cause us – the observers – to wonder, to question, to imagine and speculate on what is and what is not. It is in the nature of a child to wonder about the world around it. As children explore their surroundings they wonder what would happen if they push a button or open a door, what a dog feels like, why a plant died or how to make a bigger soap bubble. Experiencing wonder does not stop when we reach adulthood; it remains fundamental to our existence. As a matter of fact, wonder might be humankind's most important emotional expression, something we do not outgrow as adults. Nevertheless, adults have a different relationship to wonderment, as they seek a more scientific understanding of the sensory world.

*'And I said, "Gabor, if I could think what I would do, other than architecture, it would be to write the new fairy tale, because from the fairy tale came the airplane, and the locomotive, and the wonderful instruments of our minds . . . it all came from wonder."'*

Louis Kahn (Estonian-born American architect, 1901-1974)

According to our perception, that which has been seen achieves the status of 'wonder' if it is exceptional, unique and one-of-a-kind, when it stands out from the 'more-of-the-same', the 'similar-to-the-rest'. Seeing something makes us curious and prompts us to question how it was created and built. When something is wonderful we take delight in it, it makes us think it is unique, special and awesome instead of 'merely' good, which definitely would not be wonderful enough. But first and foremost it feeds our curiosity and is driven by a hunger for comprehension for its own sake.

The act of wondering creates a disruptive momentum, a spectacular interruption of mundane reality and brings us into intimate contact with the seen. For a fraction of a moment, the intimacy or closeness with the seen brings us to a standstill. It leaves us speechless, prompts a sense of doubt and perplexity, and renders all our actions and the familiar null and void. We may be briefly impressed, puzzled or intimidated by what confronts us. To be in wonder – surprised and bewildered – is an apocalyptic experience. Man-made world wonders trigger that apocalyptic experience, proclaiming the end of the world as we have known it and heralding a new world to come.

*'The larger the island of knowledge, the longer the shoreline of wonder.'*

Huston Smith (American religious studies scholar and author, b. 1939)

Wondering occurs in a highly charged space between logic, credibility and disbelief, which is what man-made world wonders should advocate and embody. The novelty and uniqueness of man-made world wonders is a function of aspects of scale, technological intelligence and great storytelling. The core drivers that make man-made world wonders are superlatives measured on scales such as size or beauty, as well as by technological intelligence and great storytelling. They produce knowledge and feed human progress for better or worse.

Man-made world wonders are the archetypes of innovation in new scales, technologies and myths. A true built wonder excels in these aspects and it remains a wonder even though we might have a perfectly logical, scientific or technical explanation for it. Such wisdom or knowledge does not abolish wonder; our explanations and theories are often more wondrous than the object itself. And with it, we unravel the endless depths of the mysteries of life.

# The Superlative in Scale

*'The essence of life is statistical improbability on a colossal scale.'*

Richard Dawkins (English ethologist, b. 1941)

Scale is our measure of all things and how we relate to them. We perceive the world around us through our senses. As the product of subjective empirical perception, scale gives measure and value to everything we see, feel, taste, smell and hear. We collectively agree on units of measurement such as metres, feet, inches, kilograms, tonnes, joules and kilometres per hour. These tangible units are tools that allow us to measure and organize the world – by length, volume, energy, force, time or some other aspect of human reality. Scale is a measure against human need, desire, interest and function. We personally or collectively add value to something in order to claim and mark its quality, preciousness and originality. Something with a higher value seems to be more important than something with a low value. Those that are highest on the scale express the highest degree of a quality within that scale and can therefore be described as superlatives. Superlatives such as most, first, best, longest, highest, tallest and largest (and their opposites) are indicative of man-made world wonders and those that will be created in the future. The superlatives of any scale challenge us to enter into a new relationship with the world and our built environment.

*'You can often measure a person by the size of his dream.'*

Robert H. Schuller (American televangelist, b. 1926)

By organizing the world in measurable aspects of reality, we position ourselves within the theory of measuring and scaling, us and the other, more and less, big and small, truth and falsehood, beautiful and ugly, precious and worthless. Values of scale make us compare, understand, assess, hierarchize and rank, make us choose, select and evaluate, and they can likewise create enthusiasm and disgust, passion and ignorance. We define scale and then scale defines us, separating us from the rest, from the ordinary or common. Scale expresses an attitude and creates competition.

Scale is the product of our relationship with the earth, the micro- and macrocosm, the objects we surround ourselves with, the universe and beyond. It provides order. It creates logic, provides contrast and sharpens our view of how life and the world around us work.

Scale produces personal as well as collective meaning and offers benchmarks; it is the core driving force for the creation of man-made world wonders. Unconsciously we compare and put everything into hierarchies of scale. Those places, objects or buildings that score highly or perform exceptionally within these hierarchies of scale, the superlatives, are the ones we label as world wonders.

*'A great building must begin with the immeasurable, must go through measurable means when it is being designed, and in the end must be unmeasured.'*

Louis Kahn (Estonian-born American architect, 1901-1974)

Man-made world wonders impress us by excelling on multiple scales. They compete with old records and introduce new ones in some measurable unit. A 100-m-high building may be an exquisite work of art, but it is the highest building that will impress us most and will be noted as wondrous and visually spectacular. Reaching a height of 830 m, the Burj Khalifa skyscraper in Dubai is currently the world's tallest man-made structure, having outstripped the 630-m KVLY television transmission mast in North Dakota that previously held the record. Another man-made world wonder for its size is the Great Wall of China. With a total length of about 8,850 km it is a true superlative in the league of longest man-made structures and remains unbeaten. With regards to durability, the Pyramid of Meidum, the Bent Pyramid and the Red Pyramid in Egypt from 2580 BC are probably the oldest man-made structures still standing.

Whether superlative in height, length, volume, age or beauty, scale alone is far from sufficient to make a world wonder but it is certainly a prerequisite.

# Pioneering Technology

*'This world, after all our science and sciences, is still a miracle; wonderful, inscrutable, magical and more, to whosoever will think of it.'*

Thomas Carlyle (Scottish philosopher, 1795-1881)

Some people say technology dispels wonder, but it actually nourishes wonderment because technology of any kind transforms an idea of an object, machine or building into the actual shaping of reality and functionality. Scientific and technological excellence, along with its materialization, structure, form and composition, add up to the wonderment in the man-made.

We can design our children or extend our bodies with prosthetic elements. We manipulate the weather, condition our environment and genetically manipulate our food. We robotize and automate production and mobility processes. We reach unprecedented heights and overcome distances that are measured in light years.

Technology facilitates human development and the full realization of human potential, not as remedial action but in an attempt to go beyond what has already been achieved. Technology gives us the confidence to solve problems using creative engineering processes, which can also reveal new problems and help to tackle them. Technology brings change into actual being. It is accurate and empowers reliability. Technology gives us the feeling we are able to create and control, to manage and manipulate the planet according to our desires and our existential fears, which is what man-made world wonders exemplify. Technology gives us the confidence to take more responsibility in our honest attempts to make our lives more bearable, safer, more comfortable, more hopeful – less uncertain and maybe more meaningful.

Man-made world wonders are symbols of technological skill and power. They are constructed by pioneering science and technology and search beyond the bounds of widely acknowledged limitations, proudly representing the latest technological achievements and the power of ingenious human creation. They show an appetite for risk and experimentation as they seek to challenge the laws of nature. They play with and manipulate the spectators' senses, driving them away from the steady, predictable quality of the mundane and familiar.

Man-made world wonders bring the fictional, our dreams and fantasies closer to reality, taking away some of the uncertainty in life. They speculate beyond our technological frontiers, inspire us anew, and champion novelty and ingenuity, qualities of the unfamiliar that are still uncommon. They advocate hope and feed our dreams with confidence in a better future to come. They spur change and bring progress to society and the man-made environment. They bear witness to the post-natural world that humans are currently developing towards and contribute to our confidence, trust and belief in the future.

Man-made world wonders enforce an experience of compelling openness, which reveals and propels us into new possibilities. They outsmart any form of impossibility or uncertainty. They embrace science as well as fiction, bring them together and feed the inspiring myths of our times that are fundamental to humankind's survival. Those that stand out, pioneer and challenge the new, can be labelled as man-made world wonders, they lead us and continue to inspire us for more stories to come. Man-made world wonders reflect a high level of technological intelligence and provide further proof for the feasibility and constructability of the world yet to come.

# Great Storytelling

*'There is no longer any such thing as fiction or nonfiction; there's only narrative.'*

E.L. Doctorow (American author, b. 1931)

*A Short History of Myth*, the 2006 book by Karen Armstrong, opens with a statement: 'Human beings always have been mythmakers.' There is obviously nothing more human than the urge to speak and tell great stories. We tell stories about who we are, who we want to be and what matters to us. Everyone is a storyteller. Some tell better stories than others, but the substance of all our stories reflects the wonder of existence in a cruel but beautiful and mysterious world. Besides being storytellers we are also readers and listeners; we absorb and often believe the stories that surround us; sometimes we even become followers.

Storytelling bridges the many worlds inside people's minds. And translating these worlds into reality, into the physical world, could be called architecture, the stories of inhabiting spaces that force us all to become users. Architecture and the city, the accumulation of buildings, are stories with motives that capture the essentials of the human drama of inhabiting space and the attempt of survival within it. Architecture embraces a sequencing of events in which we temporarily become characters in scenes. These stories told by the language of architecture have a huge impact on our lives, as they tell us the story of how to behave, manoeuvre, navigate, use and inhabit a space. Architecture is also a décor that tells us the story of practicalities, which lies in fulfilling the physical need of shelter, and tells a tale of technological implications, structure, style, passion and beauty.

*'The world is full of magic things, patiently waiting for our senses to grow sharper.'*

W.B. Yeats (Irish poet, 1865-1939)

Armstrong explains that these stories, our self-created myths, enable us to 'live more intensely within the world', rather than 'opting out of this world'. Myths bind us to the world around us and we perform the events of our lives within the mythology we create.

Whether they are couched in words, pictures or architecture, myths are stories told by humans that reaffirm our very existence, are reflections of our perception and the empirical world. According to Karen Armstrong, a myth tells us 'how we should behave' and puts us 'in the correct spiritual or psychological posture for right action, in this world or the next'. Myths give us a reason to execute our lives in a humane setting ¬– or at least in one that we believe to be humane – namely the city. The city and its architectures are a physical realization and materialization of many myths, old and new, which come together. Cities reflect the ongoing myth in which we live, love, understand, make ourselves comfortable, find enjoyment and die.

Stories told in architectural language encapsulate myth and the eternal conflict between opposing themes: sinner and saint, hero and villain,

forbidden lust and unconditional love. They embrace mystery, adventure, magic and wanderlust, divine energies such as love, compassion empathy and equanimity, and the eternal battle to overcome our own demons of anger, hostility, guilt, shame and fear.
So the stories we choose to follow, realize and inhabit had better be good ones!

*'Mystery creates wonder and wonder is the basis of man's desire to understand.'*

Neil Armstrong (American astronaut, 1930-2012)

Man-made world wonders reinforce existing myths and can also demystify them, while creating powerful new stories that reframe our life journey and our relationship with the planet.
Man-made world wonders embody these outstanding creative processes and empower us with knowledge and confidence to take responsibility for the things we create, for the environments we compose, and the architectures we construct and inhabit. Man-made world wonders empower the perpetual myths and secrets of human existence and achievements, thus nourishing the mystery of above-average human existence: the supernatural. They are the keepers and re-presenters of human legacy and possess the characteristic of advocating a wonderful and exceptional, exaggerated or idealized narrative on love, beauty and despair that makes us believe in old and new mysteries of human life and endless possibilities to create.
Everything we create – objects, buildings, brands, cities and environments – is an encapsulation of myths. The myth is etymologically related to words such as mother, matrix, time, measurement, music, matter, meter, mata and mater. Myth is the womb of creation through which the infinite becomes quantified and finite in the world of space-time and causality. Myth as story reveals the creative process itself.
We need to dare to tell great stories about love, death, survival, beauty and victory, about the vices and virtues of human life. We therefore need to reclaim and embrace the spiritual in the things we create, the environments we shape and the architectures we erect.

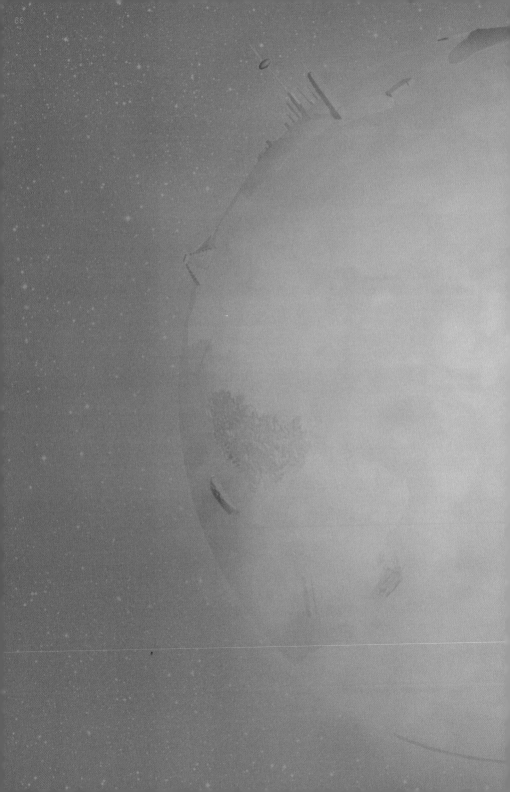

# How Can Imagination Be Explored?

Tihamér Salij

# Translating Traditional Vocabulary of Wonderment

*'The future belongs to those who believe in the beauty of their dreams.'*

Eleanor Roosevelt (former First Lady of the USA, 1884-1962)

Man-made world wonders are a testament to the spirit of wondering and how we try to understand and answer the questions we are continuously confronted with. Have we unlearned how to wonder – and how to provoke wonder? Can we still make world wonders? Can we imagine a world full of wonders? How can we explore the timeless human desire for wonder and wonderment? How can we translate the traditional vocabulary of wonderment – words like love, fear, hope, beauty, universality, perfection, precision, sublime, despair, mysterious, lightness, allure, the crazy and fantastic –

into twenty-first-century thinking? And how can we produce buildings, structures and environments with this new lexicon?
What scales and superlatives, technologies and myths will the next generation of man-made world wonders be comprised of?
What will we marvel at next? Where on the globe could new wonders emerge?
Can we articulate the visions that our societies and technologies are already poised to realize, but also imagine new fascinations, follow new dreams, define new records to beat, take further responsibility for the environment, and speculate about the structures that architecture could offer us in the future?

Man-made world wonders have traditionally been listed and categorized as tombs, temples and shrines, palaces, fortifications, statues and monoliths. Their locations mark the epicentres of historical power around the globe. Man-made wonders are in fact symbols of a higher state of consciousness that allows us to tap into the collective imagination and our collective longing to accomplish the extraordinary. They lift us to heights of passion and ecstasy. However, to take a step forward and add to the lists of man-made world wonders, categories such as connectors, weather machines, purifiers, protectors, energy generators, the extra-terrestrial, transformers and society adjusters are probably the more appropriate and passionate clusters in which future man-made world wonders will be accomplished, telling new myths and replacing old ones, allowing for new collective dreams and providing new technological solutions to protect and comfort us. The old categories are outdated.

Connectors imagine a hyper-global connectivity that transcends distance and speed.

Weather machines create, control and manipulate weather phenomena and modify the climate regionally and locally.

Purifiers are responsible for cleaning air, water and soil, filtering all the pollutants that harm the environment.

Protectors are meant to safeguard life and the environment from serious threats and total extinction.

Energy generators continue our dream of believing and innovating in energy abundance.

Extra-terrestrials promote the hyper-artificial

and alter our view of the cosmos, exploring new territories beyond earth, extending life and opening up new dimensions in space and time. Transformers introduce dynamism into architectural engineering, to produce buildings that are intangible, illusionary and adaptive, constantly morphing their shape, colour and function.

Society adjusters prompt societal change around the globe and promote a higher state of consciousness, advocating alternative political systems and new world orders.

# The Journey

*'You are an explorer, and you represent our species, and the greatest good you can do is to bring back a new idea, because our world is endangered by the absence of good ideas. Our world is in crisis because of the absence of consciousness.'*

Terence McKenna (American philosopher and author, 1946-2000)

Can we make the world more wondrous, condition and control the planet to preserve and extend the beauty of life by usurping new spaces and empowering new myths? What man-made world wonders can we imagine and what kind of wonders is our world calling for? What are the current limits of our dreams and what are our technological capabilities? Will the superlatives of tomorrow be longest, fastest, largest, smartest, highest, smallest, most compelling or most beautiful? What superlatives will we be working with? And which technological and mysterious characteristic will provide the basis for the new myths to be told? Which man-made structures hold new myths and can express them in the most magnificent and awe-inspiring way?

This exploration dives into the (im)possibilities of creating beyond our current knowledge of the laws of nature, physics and geometry. It searches for dreams old and new, the fascinations and fantastications of humankind, prompting a dialogue with contemporary science, technology, literature and art. It unlocks some of the secrets of future civilizations and showcases some of its architectural embodiments, from the scale of the extra-terrestrial to the interior world of our bodies, from macro-cosmos to micro-cosmos. Can we take elevators to outer space on a daily basis to escape to other planets and make them inhabitable? Can an artificial sun generate light and energy 24/7? Can we make invisible cities? Or an ultimate universal protection shield? A machine capable of controlling weather? A war zone that removes killing from civil life or an ever-changing public space that reacts to evolving programmes and adapts to the desires of its users? Can we clean up our universe and remove all space debris, and can we harvest minerals and energy from other planets and outer space? Or grow our cities from plants and trees by making use of genetic engineering? Can we elevate paradisiacal islands and prevent them from disappearing? Can we store all of the information in the world in a tiny chip? Can we create a super-library that literally injects all desirable knowledge into our bodies?

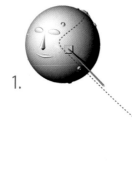

1.

2

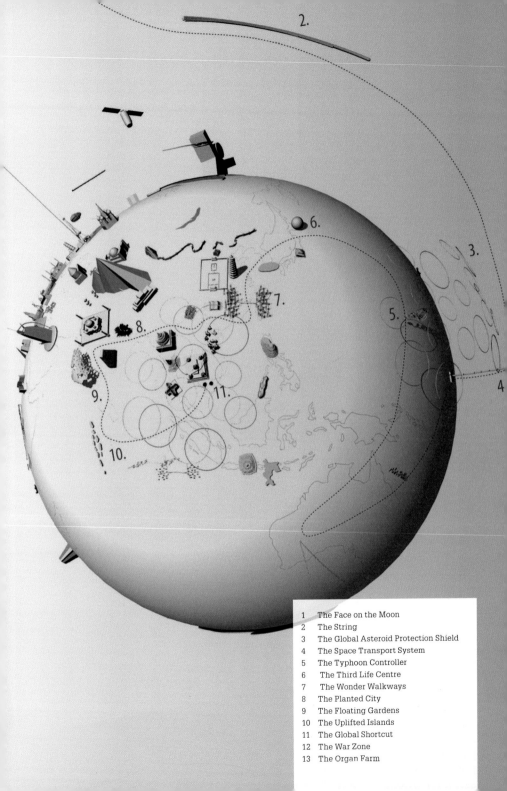

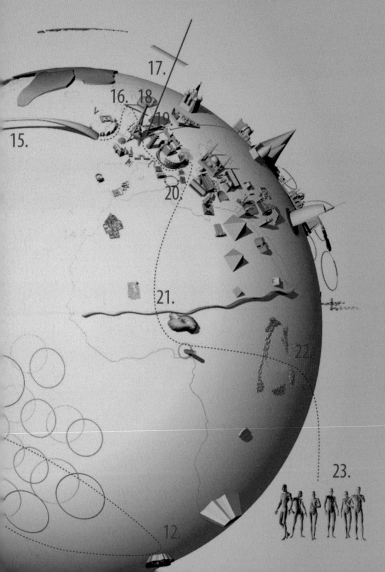

14.

15.

16.

17.

18.

19.

20.

21.

13.

11.

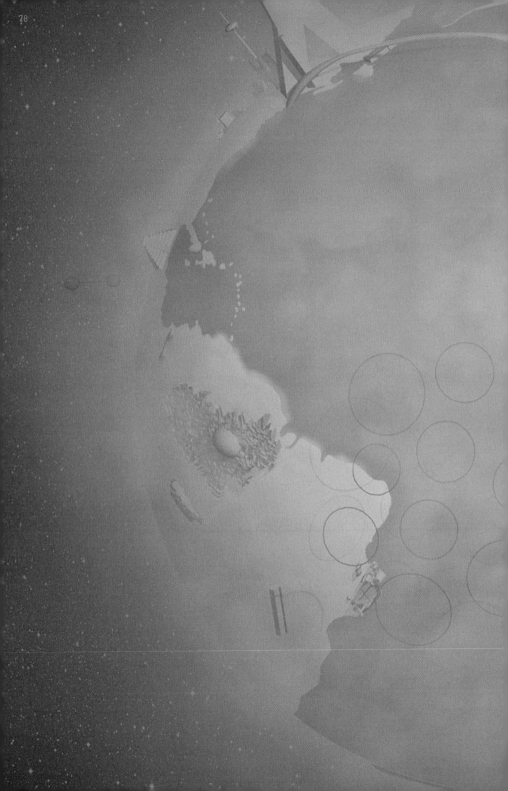

# Tomorrow's Possible Wonders?

Based on The Why Factory Studios

## 'Everyone is a moon, and has a dark side which he never shows to anybody.'

Mark Twain (American author, 1835-1910)

# The Face on the Moon

**Facts:**

| | |
|---|---|
| Classification: | Extra-Terrestrial |
| Programme: | Sculpture, memorial |
| Client: | Unknown |
| Location: | Moon |
| Size: | Surface area of sculpture: 1,075,000 m² |
| Construction time: | 19 years |

Who is that woman looking down at us? Nobody knows the person who drilled the perfect lines and carved holes into the surface of the moon. Together these lines and carvings form the face of a woman. Is she beautiful? Ugly? Does she look pained, sad or content? The maker of this sculpture must have idolatrously loved and worshipped that woman to create such a huge monument.

The story goes that a man bought a large piece of land on the side of the moon that faces the earth (the near side) and started to sculpt the biggest memorial ever made.

The surface of the moon is rocky and covered with craters. Mountains and hills surround the edges of large, flat plains. The lunar mountain ranges rise to heights of up to 7.8 km, comparable to the highest mountains on earth. In general lunar mountains are not very steep. The existing landscaping, the positioning of the craters and mountains, laid the basis for the rough features of the face. We see amazing variations of light and dark, which together shape the face of a woman. But how do you turn a lunar landscape into a fine work of portrait art? Some people say the maker lived on the moon his entire life and created the sculpture using explosives to create the craters and large chasms he needed to build up the shape of the face.

The face is famous throughout the world. For most people the sculpture represents universal values and standards. People started to tell stories about the woman who was constantly observing earth. She is 'keeping an eye on us during night time,' they say. 'She sees if one does right or wrong.'

Some people call her 'mother of all', others 'Maria', because the darker areas, the smooth lava fields created by ancient volcanic eruptions on the near side of the moon, are known as Maria (literally 'seas'; the singular is Mare). Others call her 'the goddess', but no matter what people call her she certainly became famous and loved by almost everyone.

*'I don't think the human race will survive the next thousand years, unless we spread into space.'*

Stephan Hawking (English physicist and cosmologist, b. 1942)

# The String

**Facts:**

| | | |
|---|---|---|
| Classification: | Extra-Terrestrial | |
| Programme: | Residential, agriculture, industry | |
| Client: | The New Beginning Foundation | |
| Location: | 900 km LEO-based sun-synchronous orbit | |
| Size: | Length | 60 km |
| | Diameter | 5 km |
| | Total surface area | Residential: 1,398,488,888 m² |
| | Industry / Storage: | 1,507,200,000 m² |
| | Agriculture: | 1,904,933,333 m² |
| Orbiting speed: | 14-16 terrestrial orbits per day | |
| Visibility: | Best between sunset and sunrise | |
| Layout: | 3 rings (residential, agriculture, storage / industry) | |
| Total Population: | 1,887,960 | |
| Population Density: | 2,702 km² | |
| Gravity control: | 1 G in residential ring with 0.6 rpm and radius of 1.8 km | |
| Labour: | 450,000 robots, 135,000 architects / engineers | |
| Construction time: | 75 years for 60 km (construction ongoing) | |

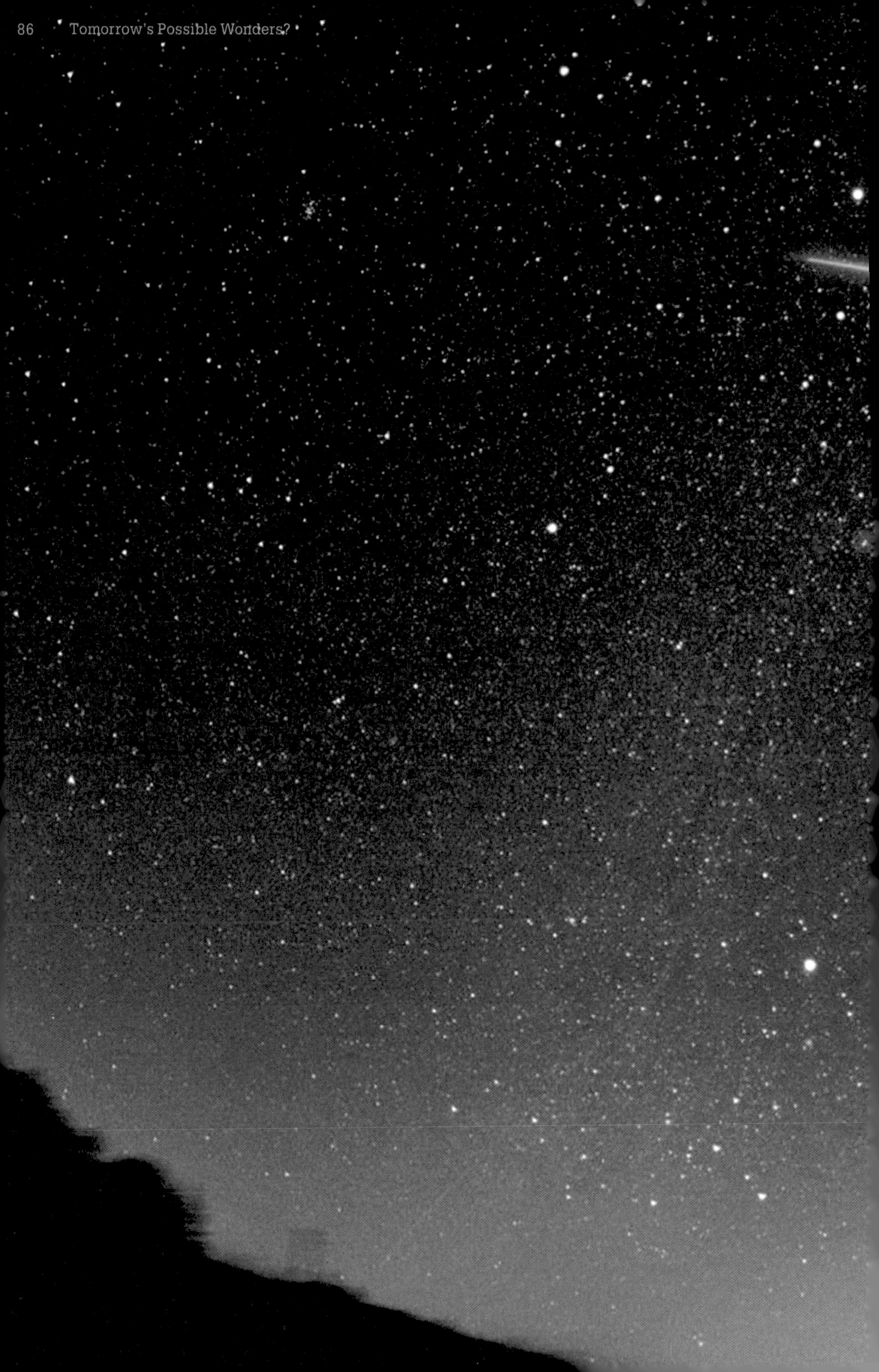

The String is a satellite city and accommodates almost 1.89 million inhabitants along its 60-km length. The String orbits at an altitude of 900 km in a sun-synchronous orbit in order to be constantly exposed to direct sunlight. The String revolves around the earth about 15 times in 24 hours and is easy to spot from various locations depending on its orbital path over the year. It consists of doughnut-shaped rings, each of which contains three different layers of programme, artificially creating an earth-like habitat. Each ring accommodates 157,330 inhabitants. The doughnut-shaped rings are docked onto a tube, which connects the habitats and supports inter-satellite traffic. The rings rotate at a circumference speed that generates an earth-like gravitational force of 1 G.

For a long time, the International Space Station (ISS), which could accommodate a maximum of 12 people, was by far the biggest and brightest of all of the man-made objects orbiting earth. For years the ISS was fun for many people to spot, but with the String a new vast star has been born. This new glowing star has literally altered our image of the heavens and made us aware of the fact that there is a real escape from earth.

The first 60 km of the String took about 75 years to construct. The String is still expanding due to increasing extra-terrestrial emigration. It took 75 years for a labour force of 135,000 architects and engineers and 450,000 robots to complete the first phase. Some 250,000 robots were specialized in construction and 3D printing, and 200,000 were specialized in mining and harnessing resources from space debris. The String can be regarded as the biggest construction site ever, a huge assembly line with the largest legion of construction robots. The robots are controlled and tele-piloted by the engineers and architects. These robots are capable of locating and navigating themselves on a construction site, executing a complex construction task and at the same time monitoring their fellow robots, with which they exchange necessary information to ensure proper execution of their individual construction tasks. Each robot can be tele-piloted manually from a maximum distance of 10,000 km. To work within the tolerances necessary for construction, tele-piloting requires accurate positioning systems and optimum communications reliability to supply data directly to the machines doing the work and vice versa. The system that has been developed for this comes from quantum computational technology and the process is called quantum entanglement, which essentially means an instantaneous teleportation of information, with the same information appearing at two different locations simultaneously. This system makes real-time activities such as the tele-piloting of robots at great distances feasible and accurate. This method of tele-piloted on-site construction gives a whole new meaning to robotics and 3D printing systems.

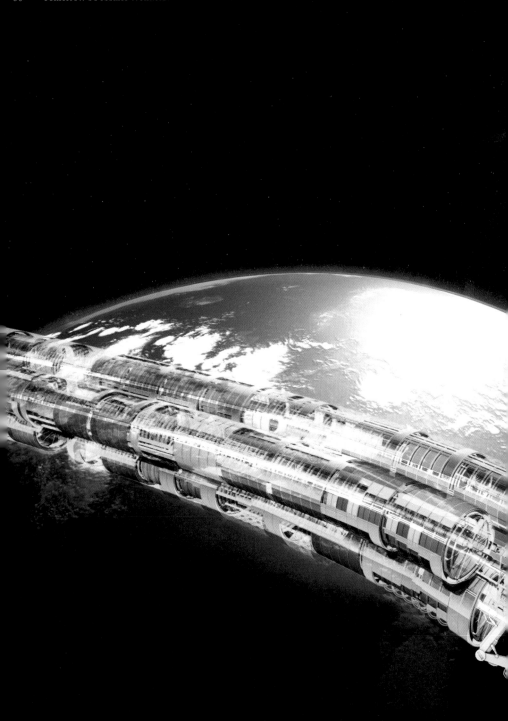

Directly linking the human task of engineering to on-site operations at a great distance has been the key to the successful completion of the String's first construction phase in a relatively short period of time. The material from which the String is made comes from space debris in the vicinity. Mining robots harness resources such as water and various metals from near-earth asteroids. They assimilate the primary resource by pulverizing it and supply the construction robots with the materials required for on-site 3D printing processes.

'After once having made
the mistake of watching
television news, I had worried
for a while about an asteroid
hitting the earth and wiping
out human civilization.
The anchorwoman had said
it was not merely possible but
probable. At the end of the
report, she smiled.'

Dean Koontz (American writer, b. 1945)

# The Global Asteroid Protection Shield

**Facts:**

| | |
|---|---|
| Classification: | Protector, Extra-Terrestrial |
| Programme: | Protection shield |
| Client: | GAPS with investments from crowd funding |
| Location: | LEO Orbit, with an operational altitude between 600 and 1,200 km |
| Size: | Minimum diameter: 0.8 km |
| Maximum diameter: | 3.2 km |
| Number of orbiting rings: | 150 |
| Construction time: | 6 years |

GAPS stands for the global asteroid protection shield, which has been constructed to eliminate asteroids and comets that threaten to hit or come too close to earth.

GAPS is designed and constructed by space scientists and experts from global disaster management authorities. It is a satellite system that can locate, track and map as many near-earth objects (NEOs) as possible. The system is equipped with a hyper-sensitive sensor system that can hear any whisper and locate a crumb anywhere and at anytime in the universe. The system is able to protect us from threatening meteorites and unidentifiable objects heading towards earth. It also cleans up space debris, including our own waste, which circulates in near-earth orbits and could pose a threat.

People call them the jellyfish of the sky, due to their form and transparency as well as their elegant movement when they are in stand-by mode.

An ion propulsion system accelerates and positions the elliptical frames. These so-called Ion Thrusters draw their electrical power from solar panels instead of burning fuel or using a conventional nuclear power source.

They are hyper-agile and can literally catch meteorites at speeds reaching tens of thousands of kilometres per hour from various orbits up to 1,200 km from earth.

The elliptical frame is made of ultra-lightweight carbon nanofibre that is filled with an ultra-strong elastic membrane. The GAPS controls the meteorite by adapting to its shape and size and then wrapping itself around half the meteorite's mass to reduce its speed and alter its pathway. It then steers the meteorite so that the burning momentum is extended when it enters earth's atmosphere, ensuring that it is completely incinerated. With this 'belt', the meteorite becomes a harmless, steerable dirigible object.

'It is good to renew one's wonder,' said the philosopher. 'Space travel has again made children of us all.'

Ray Bradbury (American science-fiction writer, 1920-2012)

# The Space Transport System

**Facts:**

| | |
|---|---|
| Classification: | Connector |
| Programme: | Infrastructure, elevator |
| Client: | NASA with various stakeholders from the Space Industries |
| Location: | Earth station (Skyhook Platform): Pacific Ocean to LEO |
| Moon station: | Lagragne Point 1 to Moon |
| Size: | Length of space elevator: 35,000 km, average length of total connection: 382,500 km |
| Construction time: | 18 years |

Writers, scientists, engineers and many others have helped to refine the space elevator over the last century. The dream of the space elevator has been made possible thanks to commercial efforts and strong governmental support from countries with leading space exploration programmes.

With an average speed of about 1,800 km per hour, a small container with a capacity of up to 50 passengers crawls up a tether towards the stars. Incredibly fast, it is nevertheless a gentle ride that takes about 19 hours to reach the first stage in the journey, an intergalactic station in geosynchronous orbit at an altitude of 35,000 km. The elevator continues its journey with its own propulsion system, using tethered movement in order to change orbits and gain altitude towards Lagragne Point 1, where it reconnects to a tether that is fixed to the moon's surface. The space elevator's cable is made from material that is very strong but low in density in order to withstand the high tensile stress.

A fixed tether takes over for the bumpy and more thrilling ride at Lagragne Point 1 near the moon.

The elevator is fully booked, 24 hours a day, 365 days a year. With the realization of the space elevator, which connects earth with the moon, a new era has started, the era of gravities. Our adaptation to various gravities will revolutionize our daily lives. New medical and commercial products will emerge from zero-G and low-G research and development, (en)lightening our existence.

'A change in the weather
is sufficient to recreate
the world and ourselves.'

Marcel Proust (French novelist, 1871-1922)

# The Typhoon Controller

**Facts:**

| | |
|---|---|
| Classification: | Protector, Climate Adjuster, Energy Generator |
| Programme: | Weather Machine |
| Client: | Governmental Pact between Japan, China, Philippines, Vietnam, South Korea, Australia and New Zealand |
| Location: | Philippine Sea, North Pacific Ocean |
| | Continent Asia |
| Machine Size: | Diameter  35m |
| | Height      30m |
| Number of machines: | 8 |
| Construction time: | 12 years |

The occurrence of a typhoon is a necessary process on which all forms of life depend and to which all forms of life adapt and evolve. Typhoons clean the air and produce huge amounts of oxygen, prevent ocean acidification, and increase biodiversity in the oceans by reducing the temperature of seawater and mixing the water layers. However, besides these environmental and ecological advantages, typhoons also have a destructive power when they become too powerful and hit human settlements.

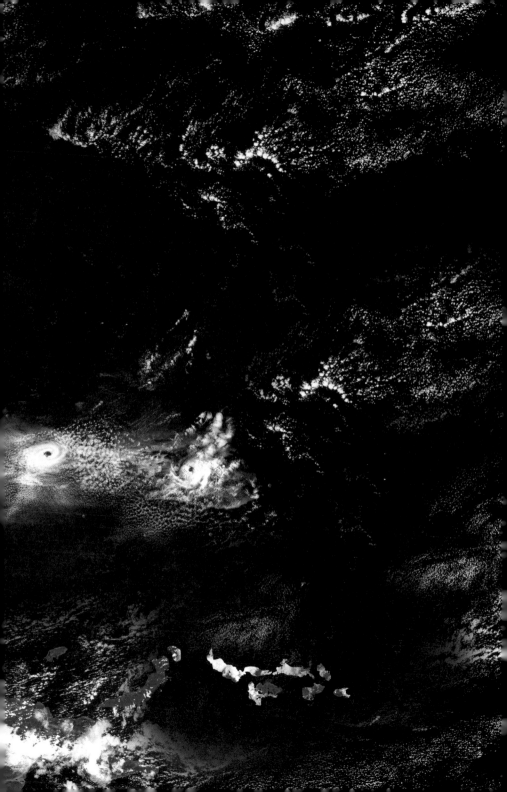

The Typhoon Controller is a collection of machines designed to influence the movement and direction of typhoons and mitigate their destructive power by reducing their wind speeds to less than 50 knots. The system is capable of steering the typhoon along a pathway that avoids harm to human settlements, infrastructure, property and human lives.

This involves a combination of smart technologies such as cloud seeding, satellites in near-earth orbit that beam microwave radiation close to or into active storms to heat the sea and air around typhoons, and spreading biodegradable oil in the pathway of typhoons to reduce evaporation to alter their paths and dissipate their power and energy.

'What is reality, anyway?
Just a collective hunch.'

Lily Tomlin (American actress and comedienne, b. 1939)

# The Third Life Centre

**Facts:**

| | | |
|---|---|---|
| Classification: | Connector, Society Adjuster | |
| Programme: | Virtual gaming centre | |
| Client: | Global Gaming Association | |
| Location: | City | Tokyo |
| | Country | Japan |
| | Continent | Asia |
| Size: | Diameter | 1 km |
| | Height | 980 m (free height) |
| | Volume | 520,000,000 m³ |
| Number of users: | 1,750,000,000 users worldwide | |
| Visitor capacity: | 270,000 | |
| Construction time: | 7 years | |

In 1748 the visionary French architect Étienne-Louis Boullée designed his Cenotaph for Newton as a visual spectacle, a giant sphere punctured by holes that create the illusion of suspended stars, while here in the twenty-first century this Third Life Centre provides shelter for those who wish to escape from gravitational reality into virtual weightlessness. With a diameter of almost 1 km, the size of this Boullée-like structure is astonishing, exceeding any realized or imagined spherical buildings and embodying the ultimate simulator of virtual reality. The Third Life Centre is a true gaming centre.

The shape of this building represents the magnificence of a perfect spherical form and symbolizes a perfectly integrated, futuristic metropolis pulsating with life, rhythm and virtual landscapes. This sphere caters to an advanced civilization that understands life and survival of the fittest by connecting it to the illusion of the virtual world. Time in the Third Life Centre becomes a vague, non-existent dimension.

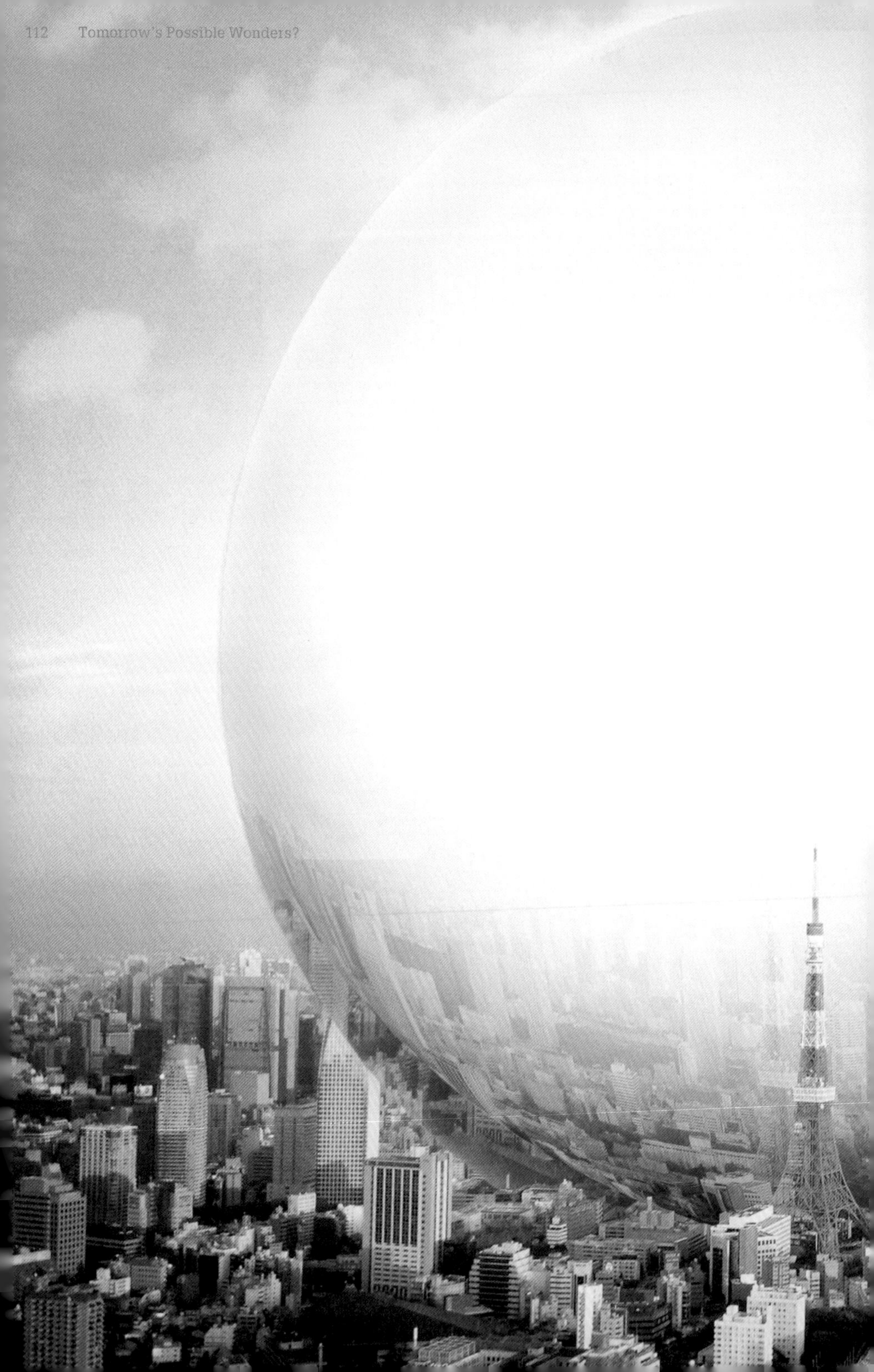

The Third Life Centre is located in Tokyo, in a region prone to earthquakes. The spherical construction is therefore made of a self-healing organic metal coating that combines optimum mechanical strength and the capacity to self-heal. The self-healing material used is inspired by nature and is in fact the artificial counterpart of a tree, which can heal damage to its trunk or branches by itself. Cracks and other damage that could arise due to earthquakes with a magnitude as great as 7 on the Richter scale disappear more or less spontaneously. A small proportion of the material's atoms move towards any cracks to fill them. The entire process of self-healing is a combination of detection and repair. The material can 'sense' that it is damaged and responds to this damage immediately.

The Third Life Centre is filled with over 520 million l of nano-liquid and can accommodate up to 270,000 visitors, which makes it the biggest aquarium and gaming centre on the planet.

Users wear gear that looks like a diving suit and are released in the bowl filled with nano-liquid, which provides weightlessness and numbness. The suit is made from a hyper-intelligent textile with a sensory system that connects the user with the nano-liquid, which induces a coma and connects the user's brain and senses to the virtual world of Third Life. The nano-liquid takes control of all senses and replaces real information with information from the virtual world that the user is connected to.

'But the beauty is in
the walking – we are betrayed
by destinations.'

Gwyn Thomas (Welsh novelist, 1931-1981)

# The Wonder Walkways

**Facts:**

| | | |
|---|---|---|
| Classification: | Connector | |
| Programme: | Pedestrian bridge, elevated pedestrian network | |
| Client: | Development Bureau of Hong Kong | |
| Location: | City | Hong Kong |
| | Country | China |
| | Continent | Asia |
| Size: | Total length | 4.6 km |
| | Highest point | 120 m |
| | Glass thickness | 1.2-3 m |
| Material: | Fibre-reinforced glass that is moulded in situ | |
| Construction time: | 4 years | |

With a sheer drop of 120 m visible beneath your feet, walking across this glass bridge is not for the faint-hearted. This bridge tests whether the users have 'nerves of steel', but also offers a spectacular view on either side towards Hong Kong Island and Kowloon. The visual effect of looking down while crossing the bridge is dramatic; only the bravest will venture the traverse. On both sides of the city the bridge continues to connect all prominent areas of the districts above street level.
It gives a surreal picture of the city, with people hovering above you while you are at street level.

The bridge was moulded as a single piece of specially toughened glass. It took just 48 days to pour it into the casting mould, but special treatment during the annealing process took almost 48 months in order to keep the glass free of fractures and give it the strength and quality to be self-supporting and carry the hundreds of users crossing it. A special furnace and manufacturing plant was used to control the heating and annealing processes. The cooling process was most risky, due to the serious possibility of fracturing the glass. The glass bridge is between 1.2 and 3 m thick, but is uniformly crystal-clear and transparent.

Locals call the glass bridge the 'Wonder Walkway' and it has become a new landmark for the city, attracting and challenging thousands of visitors every day.

# 'If one way be better than another, that you may be sure is nature's way.'

Aristotle (Greek philosopher and scientist, 384-322 BCE)

# The Planted City

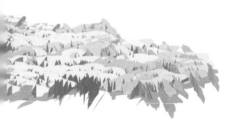

**Facts:**

| | | |
|---|---|---|
| Classification: | Transformer | |
| Programme: | Various | |
| Client: | Local inhabitants | |
| Location: | Country | India |
| | Continent | Asia |
| Size: | Village surface area | approx. 6 km$^2$ |
| | Population | 10.000 inhabitants |
| | Number of households | 3,500 |
| Material: | Bioengineered trees, plants, and tissues from animals | |
| Construction time: | Self-propagating for over 100 years (ongoing) | |

After decades of experimenting with the idea of living plant constructions, a group of biomechanical engineers together with locals in north-eastern India were able to construct a village that is made entirely of plants. The village, in its current layout, has been growing now for over 100 years and followed the existing bridge constructions, which have been there for more than 500 years. What started with bridges and prototypical buildings has grown into a fully functional village that supports about 10,000 inhabitants. Bridges, buildings, roads and even the sewage system – they all are made of living plants, trees and mixed with tissues coming from meat, muscle and bone structures to be able to create architectural details and features such as windows, doors, insulation or kitchenettes as well as sanitary objects like toilets and sinks that fit in and connect to the organic plant-like basis of the village.

Besides new technologies used in medical sciences like cell and tissue engineering, the makers of the village also made use of an old technique that makes it possible to merge indigenous plants of the same species (for example the rubber tree) into a single organism by methods similar to grafting. As a matter of fact, because the construction is alive and still growing it continues to gain strength over time and is able to increase the number of users. The village grows at a slow pace, but it is a true ecological wonder of bioengineering mixed with traditional local knowledge.

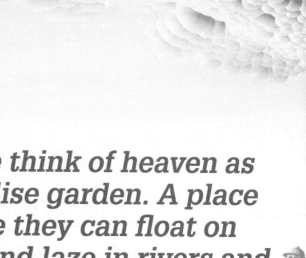

'People think of heaven as
a paradise garden. A place
where they can float on
clouds and laze in rivers and
mountains. But scenery
without solace is meaningless.'

Mitch Albom (American author, b. 1958)

# The Floating Gardens

**Facts:**

| | | |
|---|---|---|
| Classification: | Purifier | |
| Programme: | Nature, recreation | |
| Client: | Municipal Corporation of Greater Mumbai | |
| Location: | City | Mumbai |
| | Country | India |
| | Continent | Asia |
| Orientation: | Spans southwards over Mumbai from the airport to the southern coast | |
| Altitude: | between 200 and 300 m | |
| Size: | Length | 10 km |
| | Width | 5 km |
| | Surface | 24,050,000 m² |
| | Max. thickness of soil | 2–6 m |
| | Max. vegetation height | 12–15 m |
| | Max. depth of hydrogen balloon | 45 m |
| | Total weight | 3,098 megatonnes |
| Material: | Vegetation | Ironwood trees, Jamun trees, Flame of the Forest (or Parrot) trees, Tulasi plant |
| | Balloons | Polychloroprene (better known as Neoprene) with aluminium and non-flammable coatings |
| | Hydrogen | 2,613,000,000 m³ (Net force: 310,450,530,000 N) |
| Weather conditions at an altitude of 250 metres: | | |
| | Wind  Wind speed at an altitude of 300 m is 19.2 km/h (gentle breeze, Beaufort 3) | |
| | Average temperature | 27.2 °C |
| Visitors per day: | 600,000 people | |
| Construction time: | 32 months | |

With a surface area of 24,050,000 m$^2$, the Floating Gardens of Mumbai cover almost 50 per cent of the city. Like a flying carpet they add a fresh green tint to the greyness of the city, which gradually fades into the bluish sky. They move slowly, uniformly, continuously, the gardens seem to search constantly for their perfect position. Hydrogen-filled balloons that are up to 45 m high, depending on the amount of soil and flora and fauna they accommodate at a particular spot, carry a total weight of 3,098 megatonnes. This new paradisiacal territory floats above the concrete jungle of Mumbai, controlling the climate and purifying the air, but first and foremost it reinstates the city's natural character and qualities. It seems to free its architectural heaviness from its gravitational force. It introduces levitation into architectural being. Aeroponic technology mixed with pockets of highly concentrated fertile soil is used to grow the flora and attract animal life, especially large numbers of birds, insects and other small animals from the birds' food chain. It counterbalances the qualities of the concrete jungle below like a vast paradisiacal roof garden.

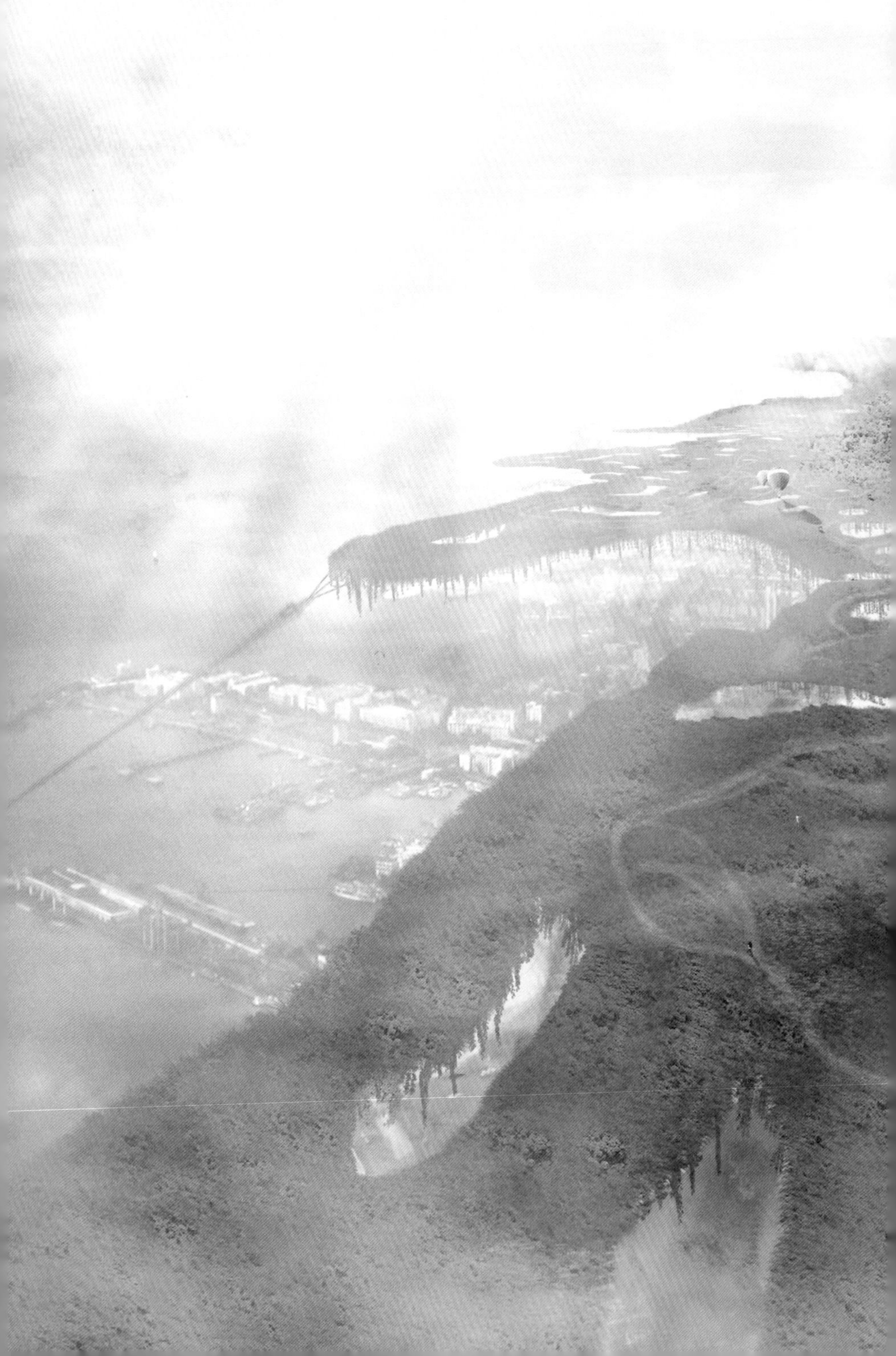

The roof is covered with typical grass and three other types of tree: the Kimshuka or Plaksha (known in English as the Flame of the Forest or Parrot tree), the Jamun tree and Ironwood tree.

The roof is composed of indigenous flora and fauna and is divided into recreational spaces, such as parks, neighbourhood gardens, and wilderness-like forests and grasslands to support larger populations of birds, rodents and other mammals. People are prohibited from entering these areas to protect the biodiversity, and digging holes is strictly forbidden. Besides having an incredible spiritual value, this green roof also represents a modern recreational and environmental facility, purifying the city's heavily polluted air while providing space for leisure activities for the citizens of Mumbai.

Alongside the indigenous flora, the roof is covered with Tulasi (known in English as Sacred Basil), which Indian people regard as one of the holiest trees because they believe it embodies the goddess Sri. Legend has it that Tulasi is, on earth, in paradise and in the netherworlds, difficult to find, so whoever wishes to reach the fruit of the four endeavours must honour Sri. Brahma, Vishnu, Siva and all other gods reside wherever a Tulasi plant flourishes; it is the meeting point of heaven and earth. In short, the tree has mystical and divine powers. Since their completion the floating gardens have transformed Mumbai into the City of Gods and has revived the tourism industry.

Openings in the roof allow for light and atmospheric control of the city below. The hanging gardens control the climatic conditions of the city of Mumbai. It balances the temperature to a mild minimum of 14 °C at night and a maximum of 30 °C during the day.

It is possible to access the 'gardens' using private and public modes of transport: airship, air balloons, cable shuttles, mini-jets and jet-packs are common means of transport and make the journey to the roof an exciting event. The roof gardens attract up to 600,000 people per day. For safety reasons the maximum number of visitors at any given moment is limited to 350,000, because of the maximum weight the roof can support.

The shell of the roof garden's 'ceiling' is covered with a highly reflective coating, to allow for extra light where needed.

'*Rising sea levels,
severe draughts, the melting
of the polar caps,
the more frequent and
devastating natural disasters
all raise demand for
humanitarian assistance
and disaster relief.*'

Leon Panetta (American statesman, former Director of the Central Intelligence Agency, b. 1938)

# The Uplifted Islands

**Facts:**

| | | |
|---|---|---|
| Classification: | Purifier, Protector | |
| Programme: | Load-bearing structure | |
| Client: | Maldives Ministry of Tourism with Ministry of Economic Development | |
| Location: | Country | Republic of the Maldives in the Indian Ocean |
| | Continent | Asia |
| | Number of elevated islands | 65 |
| Size: | Various | |
| Elevation: | 10 m | |
| Material: | 350 million tonnes of reinforced coated plastic | |
| Construction time: | 10 years | |

For centuries, the islands of the Maldives have been related to myths and catastrophic stories, such as Atlantis and Noah's Flood. These myths have been strengthened and made scientifically highly plausible by projective theories originating in climate change and global warming research. Scientists estimate that the sea level could rise by 2 or 3 m within the next 200 years. With a rise of just 0.5 m, about 77 per cent of the land mass of the Maldives would be submerged.

The Maldives government therefore considered setting aside funds from its main travel and tourism industry to finance projects that could protect the Maldives from disappearing. Another threat to the Maldives as well as to the global environment is the increasing mass of plastics filling the world's oceans: with six times more plastic than plankton floating in the middle of the Indian Ocean, the global food chain is highly polluted and fish and birds are being killed at an unprecedented rate. A million sea birds and 100,000 sharks, turtles, dolphins and whales die from eating plastic every year. Thanks to the remarkable action of the Maldives, this killing has now come to an end.

Born out of two clear threats and the desire to do something good for the global environment, the Republic of the Maldives decided to elevate 15 of its biggest inhabited islands and 50 of its uninhabited islands using plastics collected from the world's oceans. The Maldives archipelago saved itself from becoming the next Atlantis and took global responsibility for clearing the world's oceans of floating plastics. The island nation started cleaning in its own backyard, the Indian Ocean, and the cleaning of the Pacific and the Atlantic Ocean soon followed. A total of 300 million tonnes of plastics has been collected from the oceans; a further 50 million tonnes of plastics came from waste dumps all over the globe. These plastics were used for the structure needed to elevate the islands. The plastics were treated with a special coating to reinforce them and make them resistant to any form of degradation by the salt water.

A total of 65 islands have been gradually elevated at the rate of 1 m per annum, which is almost 0.3 cm per day. At this pace it has taken about ten years to elevate the selected islands by 10 m, allowing the natural environment to gradually regenerate itself and fill in any gaps.

*'Speed, it seems to me, provides the one genuinely modern pleasure.'*

Aldous Huxley (English writer, 1894-1963)

**Facts:**

| | | |
|---|---|---|
| Classification: | Connector | |
| Programme: | Tunnel | |
| Client: | Brazilian Foreign and Commonwealth Office in collaboration with the Vietnamese Foreign Policy Department | |
| Location: | | |
| | City | Rio de Janeiro, Ho Chi Minh City |
| | Country | Brazil, Vietnam |
| | Continent | South America, Asia |
| Size: | | |
| | Tunnel diameter | 26 m |
| | Length: | Normally 16,536 km, becomes c. 8,700 km straight through the earth (Source: http://www.mapcrow.info) |
| | Altitude | max. +45 m, min. -2,900 km |
| | Tunnel volume | 4,619,083,678 m³ |
| | Truckloads of excavated earth: | 230,954 (using a 20-tonne truck) |
| Materials: | | |
| | Tunnel | Reinforced carbon with a melting point of 4,915°C |
| | Vehicle | Reinforced tungsten steel with a melting point of 4,695°C |
| Construction details: | | |
| | Normal drilling machine | 20 m/day, taking 182,500 days (500 years) working in both directions |

# The Global Shortcut

| | |
|---|---|
| Drilling machine required | 2,000 m/day, taking 1,825 days (5 years) |
| Timescale | 5 years for drilling, 10 years for construction |

Vehicle:

| | |
|---|---|
| Dimensions | 16 m diameter sphere |
| Classes | Business (8 luxury seats) and General (16 seats) |

| | |
|---|---|
| Energy: | 40 gigawatt is required to power the maglev guidance system's vacuum pumps |
| General: | Gravity train supported by a maglev guidance system |
| Capacity per car | 24 people |
| Number of operating cars: | 84 |
| Capacity per day | 34,560 people |
| Train journeys per day | 1,440 one-way trips or 720 round trips |
| Lines: | 2 |
| Frequency | Round trip in 1 hour 30 minutes |
| Trains per line | 42 at a 1-minute interval |
| Speed | max. 8 km/s = 28,800 km/h |
| Duration | 42 minutes |
| Acceleration | 9.8 m/s$^2$ up to 11.4 m/s$^2$ |
| Coriolis Effect sideways speed: | max. 2,414 km/h |
| Pressure in tunnel: | max. 48,000,000 psi |
| Mantle convection speed: | 20 mm/annum, may vary closer to the core |

Travelling from Rio de Janeiro straight down to Ho Chi Minh City in 42 minutes, the Global Shortcut makes the ultimate dream of the globetrotter a reality. Spherical vehicles with a diameter of 16 m carry up to 24 passengers to the other side of the world, travelling at a speed of 28,000 km per hour. The global shortcut handles about 35,000 passengers per day on just two lines; one line per direction. The annual capacity of the Global Shortcut is 12.7 million passengers, which means that, if used to full capacity, the total population of Rio de Janeiro can travel to Ho Chi Minh City within 365 days, while the 8 million inhabitants of Ho Chi Minh City can travel to Rio within just 228 days.

The tunnels were drilled in two directions at the same time, starting from the centre of each city. At an average rate of 1,000 m per day, the drilling took almost 25 years. Drilling through the earth's crust proceeded at a relatively slow pace compared to the drilling of the upper and lower mantles and outer core. Almost half of the drilling time was used for the continental crust, due to its hard and rocky substance. Granite sometimes slowed down the tunnelling process, but the use of explosives meant that excavation of the tunnels could continue.

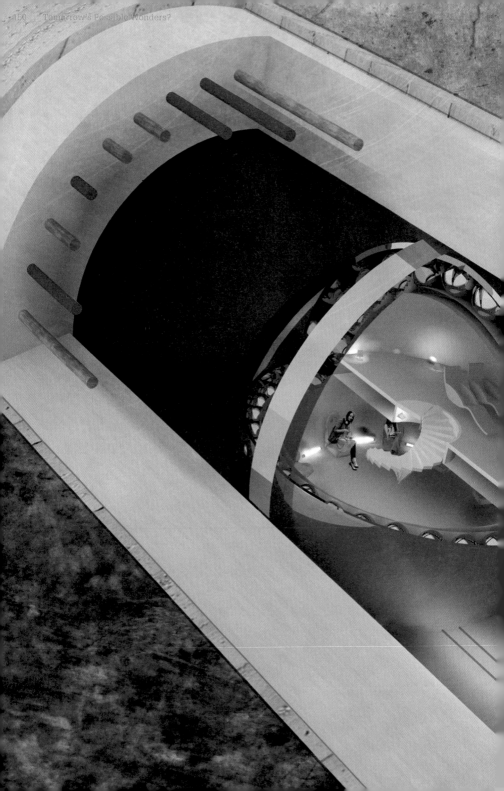

The tunnel concept combines magnetic levitation with tubes from which air is extracted to create a vacuum. Maglev technology keeps the ball afloat and in position between the tunnel walls to ensure a frictionless free fall without air resistance. With a sideways speed of 2,400 km per hour, the Coriolis Effect is greatest near the earth's core. Magnetic levitation     creates the requisite safety buffer of 0.5 m, which prevents the vehicle from being crushed against the tunnel walls due to the Coriolis Effect. Teflon tiles prevent the tunnel from melting. The tiles can withstand a temperature of over 5,000 °C and have the property of stiffening when exposed to heat, so the heat near the earth's core contributes to the tunnel's strength and stability.

The sensation of this means of travel lies in the speed and the vehicle's simple shape. The vehicle looks like a futuristic, oversized chromatic bowling ball, which can be entered through an ultra-thick safe-like door. It obviously tries to convey a sense of safety, but at the same time it evokes an uncanny claustrophobic feeling. The knowledge that each of these metal balls allows 24 passengers to pass through the earth's core at a speed of 28,000 km per hour and convey them safely to the other side of the world takes away some of the anxieties. Approaching the vehicle, which mirrors its surroundings, causes a surreal feeling. Once inside the ball, passengers sit in a specially designed, cushioned chair that provides just enough comfort to survive the free fall without it being an unpleasant experience. Facing the centre of the ball, the passenger is kept in awe and admiration, hearing only the muted fizzling of the levitational movement. The ball slowly starts to move towards the tunnel's entrance and then starts to accelerate at the speed of free fall. The inner core has an independent shell, which gyroscopically positions itself towards the direction of movement and the gravitational force. Many people take the 42-minute ride for fun, rather than to reach the destination.

'Si vis pacem, para bellum.'
(If you wish for peace,
prepare for war.)

Ancient Roman proverb

# The War Zone

**Facts:**

| | | |
|---|---|---|
| Classification: | Society Adjuster | |
| Programme: | Territory for war concentration | |
| Client: | United Nations / World Central Committee for War | |
| Location: | Artificial island floating between Bouvet Island and the Territory of the French Southern and Antarctic Lands | |
| | Country | Territory governed by the United Nations |
| | Continent | Antarctic |
| Size: | Length | 27 km |
| | Width | 15 km |
| | Highest point | 200 m |
| | Lowest point | 0 m |
| | Island surface area: | 405 km² |
| Construction time: | 23 years | |

The War Zone is a special zone located between Bouvet Island and the French Southern and Antarctic Lands about 2,500 km north of the Antarctic in which a small artificial island circulates.

The War Zone was specifically established for the waging of war. Under the auspices of the United Nations, all countries have agreed to set aside a limited territory where all conflicts and discord between nations, ethnic or religious groups can be fought out, in order to re-establish world peace and stability and exclude conflict from civil life.

Killing is the daily grind in the War Zone. Despite the moral misgivings of non-violent organizations and pacifists, this special war zone possesses a certain beauty: it has the remarkable power to eliminate killing from civil life and reduce the numbers of refugees to zero.

After the accomplishment of the dismantling of all nuclear bombs, the War Zone is the result of decades of negotiations between all countries and terrorist groups and is the only territory in which to settle a conflict in a violent way. It could be seen as a result of the last signed convention between nations and states and it completely eliminates civil death by concentrating the violence into a single designated global area. In accordance with the universal interests of humankind and the treaty that was signed by every nation, from now on every violent action outside this zone is strictly prohibited.

The legacy of the War Zone is clear: allocating space for war means peace!

In the War Zone everybody is dressed as well as licensed to kill. When nations, or any other organization representing an ethnic, terrorist or religious group or entity, decide to enrol for war, they must all sign a so-called Treaty of War, by which they agree on their desired winnings. Anybody who sympathizes with one of the parties can go to the War Zone to fight alongside them. Most wars are fought for economic or religious reasons, whether for resources or historical reasons, or for any other belief or conviction. All wars are decided within the territorial boundaries of the War Zone. The War Zone is therefore designed as an enclosure, perfectly isolated and insulated from the rest of the world. It offers several types of natural and artificial landscapes. The War Zone is a closed, controlled and regulated territory for the worst instincts and activities of humankind. The War Zone contains numerous battlefields and geographical features: mountains, flatlands, city-like environments, jungles, swamps and deserts. Every imaginable backdrop for war is offered within the territory in order to ensure technological skill and strategic intelligence, in order to allow the most diverse forms of warfare and the most advanced battle strategy. The War Zone is meant to be as diverse as possible, but the use of nuclear bombs is prohibited due to the disastrous harm it can cause to the War Zone itself and to the environment outside the War Zone territory.

The War Zone also has its own broadcasting network: radio, television and Internet offer diverse means of following and showcasing the wars. All the battles are broadcast continuously throughout the world. The War Zone Broadcasting Network is already the world's biggest network, but it still has a growing number of followers. Due to these broadcasting activities, war and the act of killing have become commercialized. War has become a real-time spectacle and has given soldiers a real face, turning them into celebrities who are admired as the gladiators of their time.

'*I suspect any worries about genetic engineering may be unnecessary. Genetic mutations have always happened naturally, anyway.*'

James Lovelock (English scientist, b. 1919)

# The Organ Farm

**Facts:**

| | |
|---|---|
| Classification | Society Adjuster |
| Programme: | Medical and clinical laboratory |
| Client: | Unknown |
| Location: | Exact location Unknown |
| | Region · Amazon |
| | Continent · South America |
| Construction Material: | skin tissue |
| Footprint: | 1,465 km² |
| Construction time: | 12 years |

The future of genetic engineering is happening here at the Organ Farm. At a top-secret location somewhere in the rainforest, a small group of scientists – including bioengineers, computational biologists and bionic designers – has established a farm that grows organs, limbs and other body parts from stem cells, nerve cells and blood cells in order to counterbalance the ongoing health crisis that is exacerbated by a shortage of organs. Besides organ farming and designing prosthetics, at the Organ Farm they aim to design the perfect drug to repair malfunctioning organs, bone structures and vessels from within the body itself.

The Organ Farm, which holds over 20,000 different types of transgenic tissues and samples, has been developed against the will of a largely represented group of medical ethicists and anti-genetic engineering activists. There are rumours that the Organ Farm has also imprisoned transgenic humans, so-called living bionic samples. In some more conservative circles the organ farm is called Monsters Nest, the Womb of Evil or Frankenstein's Villa – The Organ Farm is certainly a controversial facility. The Organ Farm looks like a huge belly that can inflate and deflate as if it were breathing. Due to the architectural appearance, it gave the region its name 'The Valley of Belly'. The Organ Farm requires self-regulating environmental conditions and secure protection against toxins and pollutants from outside, so the complete farm with its laboratories is covered by a huge dome-like structure made of skin tissue. Conventional ventilation systems were inadequate to create good climatic conditions and filters were not reliable enough to ensure constant purification. Scientists found a new way to create a stable dome-like structure and at the same time maintain the climate at exactly the same humidity and temperature throughout the farm. They developed a super-strong skin tissue that can be grown from stem cells at a speed of 1 mm per second. The samples for the transgenic skin were taken from the whale shark for strength and flexibility and from humans for temperature regulation and the perfect porous structure for filtering air. A special vascular system ensures that the skin, which is almost 7 cm thick, is kept moist. It also nourishes the skin with a special substance to keep it strong and flexible.

All kinds of limbs and organs – arms, legs, fingers and feet, ears, noses, hearts, livers, kidneys, lungs, muscles, complete eyeballs and a vast collection of over 5,000 types of skin types that vary in colour, structure and tactile sensitivity – are produced and stored under perfect climatic conditions at the Organ Farm and distributed to the rest of the world.

## 'The mystery of the universe is not time but size.'

Stephen King (American horror and science-fiction writer, b. 1947)

# The Colossus

**Facts:**

| | | |
|---|---|---|
| Classification: | Society Adjuster | |
| Programme: | Mixed use: offices, housing, leisure, recreation, airport, light industry | |
| Client: | United Nations | |
| Location: | City | New York |
| | Country | USA |
| | Continent | North America |
| Size: | Height: | 5,000 m |
| | Length: | 1,300 m |
| | Width: | 450 m |
| Materials: | 8,000 tonnes of steel, 1,300 million m$^3$ of concrete, 102,500 m$^2$ of glass | |
| Largest steel beams: | 450 m | |
| Gross Floor Area | 177,800,000 m$^2$ | |
| Weight of the structure: | 88,700 megatonnes | |
| Population: | 1.2 million inhabitants | |
| Construction time: | 15 years | |

The Colossus of New York is a record-breaking superlative when it comes to size, weight and volume. Some 5 km high, 450 m wide and 1,300 m long, the Colossus of New York dwarfs every skyscraper in the world. With its staggering 177.8 km$^2$ of programme, it is the largest mixed-use building in the world. The giant covers an area that is more than three times larger than Manhattan, which has a surface area of 57 km$^2$.

The weight of the Colossus disrupts the speed at which the earth revolves, some scientists say. At 2.5 million tonnes, mainly of stainless steel, reinforced concrete, soil for interior vegetation and laminated glass, it is the heaviest structure ever built.

The Colossus has a mixed programme distributed over 177.8 million m$^2$ of floor space. The floors are interconnected by cable car systems that travel at a speed of 8 m per second. Countless steel beams that rang e from 150 to 500 m in length ensure the structure's stability and connect the façades to the floors. The Colossus of New York is, in every regard, a building of extremes.

Of the total surface area (44.45 km²), 25 per cent is used for housing. With an average population density of 11,500 inhabitants per km², the Colossus of New York accommodates a population of 511,175 people that is distributed over its 1,100 floors. The largest 'village' is located in the upper part of the main body of the Colossus and accommodates 125,000 inhabitants. Set at a height of 3.8 km, this village enjoys wonderful views across New York City. Artificial lighting ensures perfect illumination of the village.

The Colossus houses the largest mixed programme in a single building.
It boasts excellent connections to New York City, other parts of the USA
and the world (via a fly-in airport and the many cable cars that connect
to other populous parts of the building and surrounding city).
Some of its inhabitants have never been outside the Colossus, due
to the huge, diverse programme that makes the world outside the
Colossus less interesting and attractive.
The Colossus boasts 193 shopping centres of various size, 8,900 offices
with more than 200 employees, 100 small- to medium-sized enterprises
(mainly in manufacturing) with more than 50 employees, 350 hotels,
a 700-m-long sandy beach, many recreation and sport facilities,
a baseball stadium that is home to the New York Giants, a fly-in airport,
24 IMAX cinemas, 41 parks, a concert hall for 25,000 visitors, and last
but not least, a zoo.

**Facts:**

| | | |
|---|---|---|
| Classification: | Connector | |
| Programme: | New York–London connection, wind farm, fish farm | |
| Client: | Cities of New York and London | |
| Location: | City | New York, Atlantic Ocean, London |
| | Country | Between the United Kingdom and the USA |
| | Continent | North Atlantic Ocean |
| Size: | Bridge Length | 5,571 km |
| | Tube diameter of bridge | 22 m |
| Levels: | 2 (one per direction) | |
| Tracks: | 10 (5 per level) | |
| Train length: | 10-car train of 500 m | |
| Trains per day: | 192 | |
| Frequency: | Every 15 mins in both directions | |
| Capacity per car: | 800 people | |
| Daily connection capacity: | 7,680,000 passengers per day | |
| Propulsion technology: | Magnetic levitation | |
| Acceleration: | 20 m/s$^2$ (>2 G) | |
| Train speed: | 1,400 km/h | |
| Duration of journey: | 4.15 hours | |

# The Long Span

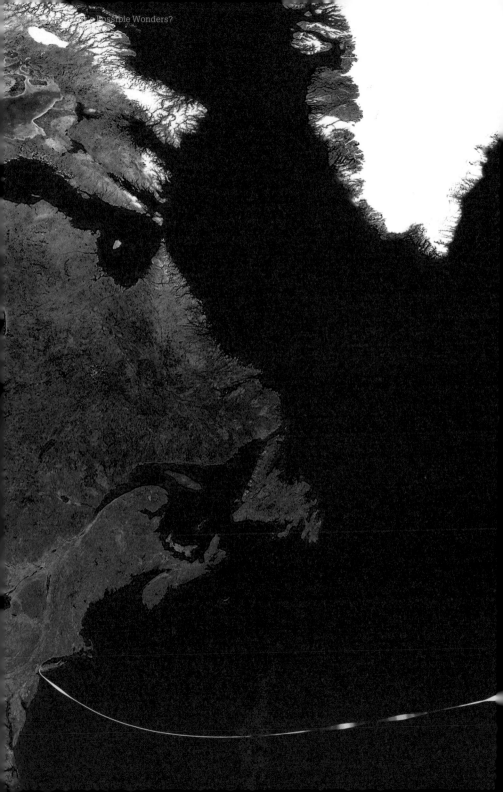

A high-speed maglev train that connects London and New York has slashed the 7.5-hour flight by conventional aeroplane to a remarkable 4-hour trip by rail.

The Long Span is a transatlantic bridge that connects two metropolises and their financial centres and at the same time enables two cities on two different continents to expand towards each other. People can easily live in London while working in New York City, or vice versa.

The ten tracks operate on two different levels, each of which operates in one direction. It caters to a total of 480 departures per day in both directions, at a frequency of 15 minutes in each direction. About 7.68 million people travel to the other side each day, which makes it the busiest railway connection on the planet. The Long Span offers unprecedented development opportunities for the two cities and their metropolitan regions, providing a boost to their economies as well as the well-being of their citizens.

*'The desire to reach for the sky runs deep in our human psyche.'*

César Pelli (Argentine American architect, b. 1926)

# The Leaning Tower

**Facts:**

| | | |
|---|---|---|
| Classification: | Connector | |
| Programme: | Mixed use, offices and housing | |
| Client: | Unknown | |
| Location: | City | Oslo |
| | Country | Norway |
| | Continent | Europe |
| Size: | Building length | 1,200 m |
| | Building height | 500 m |
| Construction time: | 7 years | |

With an incline of 25 degrees, the Leaning Tower of Oslo is the world's tallest leaning tower, at 500 m in height and 1,200 m in length.

The tower is stabilized by a structure comprised of a super-strong exoskeleton, which stiffens the shell and holds the weight of the floors. The floors, walls, columns and windows are all made of ultra-light materials. The shell of the tower, for example, is clad in large panels of lightweight layered transparent borosilicate glass. The glass layers are bound by polyurethane and polyvinylbutyral interlayer films. Walls, floors and furniture are made from specially designed high-performance reinforced cardboard materials.

More than 800 graphene cables connect parts of the exoskeleton of the building to a large concrete foundation with a dense mesh of reinforced steel, to which they are anchored to keep the building in a stable and leaning position.

Walking and standing underneath the Leaning Tower is a threatening but unforgettable thrill.

*'It is the artist's business to create sunshine when the sun fails.'*

Romain Rolland (French novelist, 1866-1944)

# The Artificial Sun

**Facts:**

| | | |
|---|---|---|
| Classification: | Weather Machine, Climate Adjuster | |
| Programme: | Artificial light source | |
| Client: | Consortium between Iceland, Denmark, Sweden and Norway | |
| Location: | Country | Iceland, Denmark Sweden, Norway |
| | Continent | Europe |
| Size: | Light structure's total size: | 64 km$^2$ |
| Number of mirrors: | 12,396 | |
| Area of the illuminated surface on earth: | 1,500,000 km$^2$ | |
| Total surface area of the mirrors: | 793,388 km$^2$ | |
| Material for mirrors: | Enhanced Aluminium MIRO 8 | |

The Artificial Sun is a huge mirror in space that can reflect light to a chosen region on earth. The Artificial Sun orbits at an altitude of 800 km. The reflector of the satellite has a surface area of about 790,000 km$^2$ when completely unfolded and is comprised of 12,400 mirror panels with a surface area of 64 km$^2$ each. The Artificial Sun illuminates an area on earth of 1.5 million km$^2$ and controls the intensity of light there. The space mirror has a slightly concave shape and the membrane is made of a thin film of special aluminium, which is able to reflect 95 per cent of the sunlight spectrum.

After decades of using primitive artificial light sources such as candles, street lights, electric light bulbs and LEDs, the Artificial Sun opens up in the morning and evening hours to illuminate daytime activities on a huge scale, thus changing the way people live and sleep in the polar regions of the Northern Hemisphere, as well as altering the ecosystems of cities and villages. The short days that inhabitants of cities like Reykjavik and Oslo are confronted with in the winter season have been consigned to the past.

The Artificial Sun alleviates the typical regional ailments, such as insomnia and depressive illnesses like Seasonal Affective Disorder (S.A.D.), which are caused by a lack of light. Depression, mental disorders and alarming suicide rates have been decreasing since the Artificial Sun started to illuminate the region. It provides extra light before sunrise and compensates with extra light after sunset in order to extend daylight hours for just a couple of hours. During the day, when the natural sun rises no higher than the horizon, the Artificial Sun increases its luminosity to attain the average daylight illumination of about 35,000 lux that people need.

# The Dancing Cloud

**Facts:**

| | | |
|---|---|---|
| Classification: | Connector, Transformer | |
| Programme: | Dance club | |
| Client: | City of Berlin | |
| Location: | City | Berlin |
| | Country | Germany |
| | Continent | Europe |
| Size: | Length: | 230 m |
| | Width: | 90 m |
| | Dome diameter: | 85 m |
| | Dome height: | 20 m |
| Surface: | 5,674 m² | |
| Altitude: | 120 m | |
| Weight: | 0.2 megatonnes | |
| Number of propellers: | 880 | |
| Capacity | 10,000 people | |
| Construction time. | 15 months | |

The Dancing Cloud turns the city of Berlin into the epicentre of world hedonism.
No longer are Bangkok, Ibiza, Miami, New York or London the cities with the most spectacularly designed clubs or party venues; Berlin has now taken the lead as the most exciting city for an exuberant nightlife.
The Dancing Cloud is a floating venue for up to 10,000 clubbers that transforms a night out into a completely new experience.
Thanks to the extraordinary experience it offers, the Dancing Cloud attracts world-class artists from all genres and makes any performance unique. Critics say artists only achieve world-class stardom from the moment they perform at the Dancing Cloud in Berlin.
Nothing beats the adrenaline and exhilaration of listening and dancing to music in a beautifully designed space that hovers above the city.

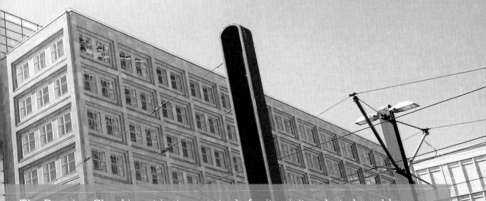

The Dancing Cloud is not just a spectacle for its visitors but also adds a spectacle to the city. It can adapt to the dancing activities and senses the mood of the crowd, translating this into movement and colours. When the crowd reaches a higher state of consciousness, the Dancing Cloud is able to gain height and move up and down at a comfortable speed while also changing its colour.

The Dancing Cloud consists of a basic structure built of lightweight carbon, which is filled with helium cushions and uses a dozen small, solar-powered engines to manoeuvre and maintain altitude. The cloud is set into operation by 25,000 spraying jets, which are dispersed over the entire object.

A highly complex technical process optimizes the spray from each of these jets. The jets receive the necessary information about local weather conditions to create a constant dense fog.

*'No one lights a lamp
in order to hide it behind
the door: the purpose of light
is to create more light, to open
people's eyes, to reveal the
marvels around.'*

Paulo Coelho (Brazilian writer and novelist, b. 1947)

# The Needle

**Facts:**

| | | |
|---|---|---|
| Classification: | Connector | |
| Programme: | Viewing tower | |
| Client: | City of Paris with a private local investor | |
| Location: | City | Paris |
| | Country | France |
| | Continent | Europe |
| Size: | Height | 1,400 m |
| | Diameter | 20 m |
| Elevator speed: | 28 m/s | |
| Elevator Technology: | Maglev technology | |
| Emitting material: | aromatic carbonyls combined with organic solar cells | |
| Construction time: | 2 years | |

The Needle reinforces the reputation of Paris as the 'City of Light' on a grand scale. It began with the gas lighting for the Champs-Elysées and wrapping the Eiffel Tower in light, but the desire of Paris to be the best-lit city in the world has not been extinguished. To some people the Needle symbolizes the start of a new period of Enlightenment, because light is a metaphor for intellectual freedom and progress towards the achievement of knowledge. To others it is merely another act of city branding, a publicity stunt aimed at attracting tourists. However, the Needle is a true highlight in structural as well as bioengineering.

The Needle reaches a height of 1,400 m and it is entirely coated with a thin foil made from organic carbon-based compound with unique phosphorescent properties for emitting light during the day as well as the night. The compound is made with aromatic carbonyls and combined with organic solar cells that mimic the natural process of plant photosynthesis to harvest energy during the day and store enough energy to glow at night. Among the self-supported viewing towers, The Needle is a unique structure and composition of the strongest available materials. The tower is rigid and stiff, but flexible enough to withstand and counterbalance the strong winds at higher altitudes. Unlike most other towers with conventional steel constructions, the base of the tower does not use a tripod-like structure. Such strengthening is unnecessary because of the use of titanium silicon carbide. The Needle has a perfectly circular shape with a constant diameter of 20 m all the way to the top. Titanium silicon carbide is a unique material that possesses qualities of ceramics as well as metals, such as high elastic modules, oxidation resistance, high bending and damage tolerance compared to other metals like stainless steel.  The base of the tower is sunk some 100 m into the ground and connected to a large foundation block of super-solid cement with a volume of 4.7 km3. Eight cables with a length of 1,400 m connect the base to the top of the Needle, where the observatory is located. The cables are made of carbon nano-tubes, a composite material with an extremely high tensile strength and a very high elasticity factor. The cables keep the tower in tension, controlling and stabilizing the swaying movements caused by wind.
The observatory platform is set at 1,400 m and has a capacity of up to 200 people, which is limited by the number of people that fit into the elevator. The elevator is the fastest in the world and is one of the tower's most amazing features. The elevator needs 60 seconds to reach the height of 1,400 m. This includes the acceleration and deceleration phases that prevent passengers being squeezed to the ceiling or floor. At high speed the elevator is capable of travelling 28 m per second. The Needle elevator's passengers feel no vibrations during travel. The vibrations, which usually occur with ordinary motor-driven elevators that are connected to a cable, are eradicated by using the magnetic levitation system. This maglev technology reduces vibration by maintaining a constant distance from the guide rail, and at the same time the magnetic suspension cushions any vibration.
The rapid change in atmospheric pressure on the non-stop ride up or down the Needle can cause an uncomfortable pressure imbalance in passengers' ears, but this effect is counteracted by an advanced air-pressure control system that adjusts the pressure in the elevator depending on its position in the shaft.
Besides the unforgettable view and choreography of lights, the elevator journey makes the Needle of Paris an unmissable experience.

'If it's invisible, I can't
remember if it's there or not.
And not only that, but I can't
even remember what it is.'

Jarod Kintz (American author, b. 1982)

# The Invisible Buildings

**Facts:**

| | | |
|---|---|---|
| Classification: | Protector | |
| Programme: | Residential, office | |
| Client: | Unknown | |
| Location: | City | Rome |
| | Country | Italy |
| | Continent | Europe |
| Size: | Invisible Tower: | |
| | Height: | 91 m |
| | Diameter: | 65 m |
| | Gross Floor Area: | 75,600 m$^2$ |
| | Construction time: | 6 years |
| | Invisible House: | |
| | Height: | 23 m |
| | Diameter: | 33 m |
| | Gross Floor Area: | 415.5 m$^2$ |
| | Construction time: | 2 years |

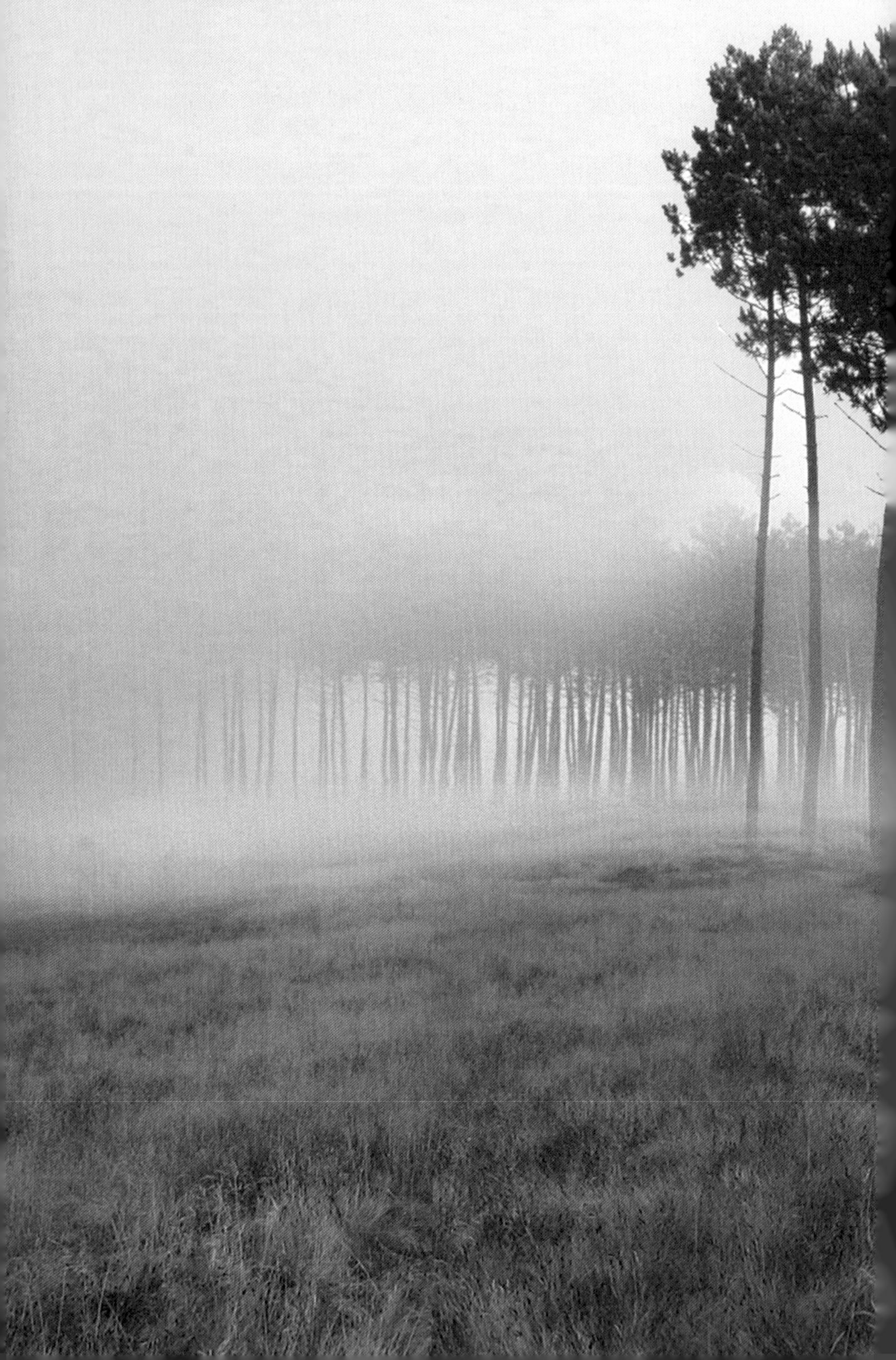

Camouflaged buildings are nothing new, but this technique has never been applied to architecture before. Neither the Invisible Tower nor the Invisible House are an optical illusion; they are buildings wrapped in a deflective skin that reveals the surrounding environment.

This intelligent skin casts no shadow and does not produce a reflection. Any light or electromagnetic wave is deflected around the area, guided by the meta-material to emerge on the other side as if it had passed through an empty space. Electromagnetic waves flow around an object hidden inside the meta-material cloak, just like water flowing virtually undisturbed around a smooth rock in a river.

These invisible buildings protect their cultural or natural heritage from modern perils. When doors and windows are closed these invisible buildings completely blend into their surroundings.

'Water, water, water...
There is no shortage of water
in the desert but exactly the
right amount...unless you try
to establish a city where
no city should be.'

Edward Abbey (American author and park ranger, 1927-1989)

# The Secluded Deserts

**Facts:**

| | | |
|---|---|---|
| Classification: | Protector, Connector, Climate Adjuster | |
| Programme: | Nature | |
| Client: | Unkown | |
| Location: | Region   Sahel | |
| Continent | Africa | |
| Size: | Length: | 13,800 km |
| | Thickness of sand wall | 5 m |
| | Height | 50 m |
| Material: | Trees, plants and 15.6 million cubes of sand | |

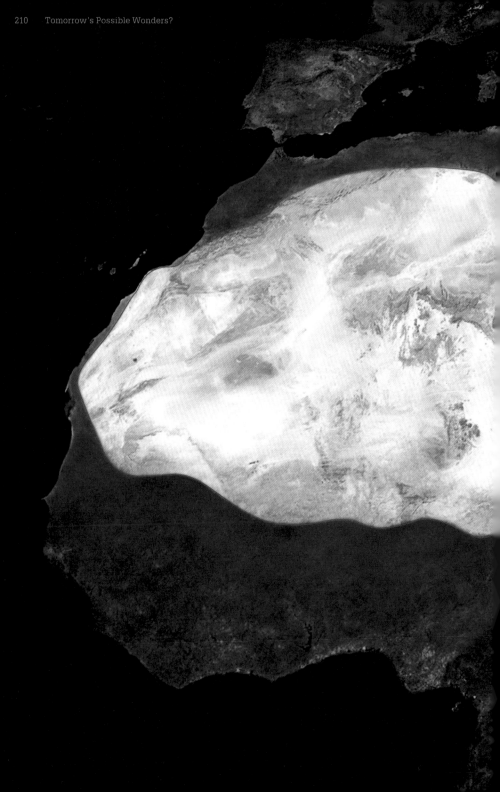

In the mid-1980s the Great Green Wall Initiative was started locally, by planting trees and increasing tree density at the edge of the threatening southward spread of the Sahara. With a total length of 13,800 km, the wall entirely encloses the Sahara desert and prevents it from growing bigger. Walls tend to socially enclose and separate, but this wall does the opposite: it has unifying qualities. Local communities and nations on both sides of the wall have benefited enormously, as has the global environment.

The wall actually consists of a strip of trees and a straight wall. The wall functions as a sand blocker and windbreaker, while the tree strip functions as a natural sand filtering system and the roots prevent soil erosion.
The wall is 50 m high and is made of stacked 5-m cubes of sand that are primed with a bacteria called BioGrout. BioGrout is an improvement method based on microbiologically induced precipitation, which increases the strength of the sand mass by creating bridges between the sand grains.
The environmental, economic and social impact of the wall is great.
It reduces land erosion, improves soil fertility, increases crop yields and improves fodder availability. It strengthens resilience to climate change, increases biodiversity and diversifies the local and regional economies of all the states surrounding the wall.

This concept of enclosing deserted regions by a smart green wall have been applied to other locations on the globe such as the Arabian desert, the Patagonian desert in South America, the Kara Kum Lut Thar desert and Gobi desert in Asia and Great Sandy Simpson desert in Australia.

'It is not light that we need,
but fire; it is not the gentle
shower, but thunder. We need
the storm, the whirlwind,
and the earthquake.'

Frederick Douglass (African American abolitionist and statesman, 1818-1895)

# The Lightning Harvester

**Facts:**

| | | |
|---|---|---|
| Classification: | Energy Generators, Society Adjuster | |
| Classification: | Energy Generators, Society Adjuster | |
| Programme: | Energy plant | |
| Client: | Partnership between Republic of Congo and Uganda with local energy companies | |
| Location: | Country | Democratic Republic of Congo, Uganda |
| | Continent | Africa |
| Altitude | 54 km from the earth's surface | |
| Size: | Length | 1 km |
| | Width | 1 km |
| | Height | 10 km |
| Material: | Grid made of graphene tubes | |
| Technology: | 260 drones spraying silver iodine for cloud seeding at an altitude of 1 km | |
| Energy production: | 66 exajoules/year = 12 % of the world's annual energy consumption of 550 exajoules in 2010 | |

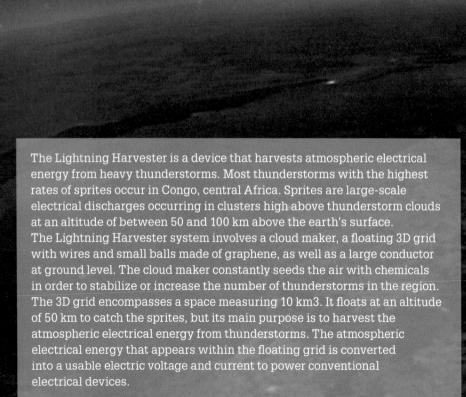

The Lightning Harvester is a device that harvests atmospheric electrical energy from heavy thunderstorms. Most thunderstorms with the highest rates of sprites occur in Congo, central Africa. Sprites are large-scale electrical discharges occurring in clusters high above thunderstorm clouds at an altitude of between 50 and 100 km above the earth's surface. The Lightning Harvester system involves a cloud maker, a floating 3D grid with wires and small balls made of graphene, as well as a large conductor at ground level. The cloud maker constantly seeds the air with chemicals in order to stabilize or increase the number of thunderstorms in the region. The 3D grid encompasses a space measuring 10 km3. It floats at an altitude of 50 km to catch the sprites, but its main purpose is to harvest the atmospheric electrical energy from thunderstorms. The atmospheric electrical energy that appears within the floating grid is converted into a usable electric voltage and current to power conventional electrical devices.

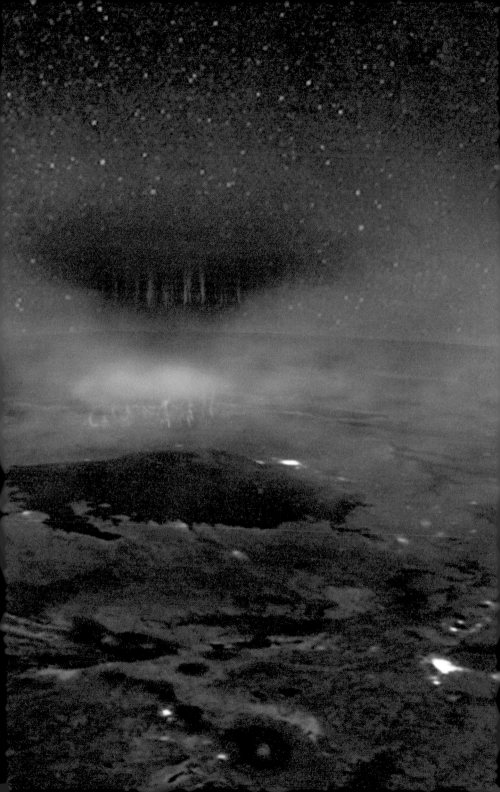

The artificially seeded dramatic cloudbursts in the area constantly release bolts of lightning, causing sprites and elves to occur at a higher altitude. The positive cloud-to-ground and cloud-to-cloud lightning flashes during the thunderstorms trigger sprites and elves.

The diversity in lightning – the rhythm, brightness and amazing colours – make the area a serious competitor for the Northern Lights, which are polar lights also known as the Aurora Borealis, after Aurora, the Roman goddess of dawn. The Northern Lights change shape, direction and colour at a slow pace, while the Lightning Harvester displays a more energetic and vivid light spectacle. Sprites appear in a diversity of jellyfish-like shapes with hanging tendrils in reddish-orange or greenish-blue hues. They can also be preceded by a reddish halo.

The Lightning Harvester attracts millions of visitors to the region every year.

*'Human knowledge and human power meet in one.'*

Francis Bacon (English philosopher, statesman and essayist, 1561-1626)

# The Super Library

**Facts:**

| | |
|---|---|
| Classification: | Society Adjuster, Connector |
| Programme: | Knowledge storage, coded DNA strings that store and transmit data |
| Client: | Unknown |
| Location: | intracellular |
| Material: | biologically based liquid |
| Size: | microscopic 0.2 nm |
| Storage capacity: | 500 petabytes |
| Data speed: | 40 petaFLOPS (Floating-point Operations Per Second) |

The Super Library's design picks up on an old human desire to gather all information in the world into the smallest space imaginable and make it accessible to everybody: libraries, computers and the Internet are good examples of this. Bioengineers developed an intra-human system to store and access information. The system uses artificial cells and its own streams of artificially encoded DNA. These cells hold information, but are also able to monitor the body for malfunctions. Active 'medi-cells' circulate around the body, recording information and comparing it to the stored data, which provides information on the ideal conditions for your body and performance. Medical care and treatment have become quicker and more efficient ever since the Super Library, also known as Bio-Net, was brought onto the market.

The Super Library marks the advent of the Age of Artificial Intelligence. The legacy of the Information Age is that DNA has become storage for natural as well as artificial information. With Bio-Net and the circulation of masses of data on a cellular level, information has become omnipresent. Bio-Net has raised some ethical and moral dilemmas, questions of right and wrong, good and bad. The boundary between knowing, interpreting and understanding has become thinner and fuzzier. Who decides what data to use and mine? Who can access and edit it? Does the injected information conflict with our human DNA? What would happen if that were the case? Will people die from an information overdose? Will information become the new drug? Will life be reduced to nothing but a script? So far it has been impossible to answer these questions.

Scientists designed artificial DNA with its own coding system because they discovered that biological DNA and its CATG coding could mutate and interfere with the human organism, which turned out to be life threatening. Accessing, selecting and reading data would also present a major problem. However, artificial DNA depends on its own coding system, so it does not interfere with the existing system.

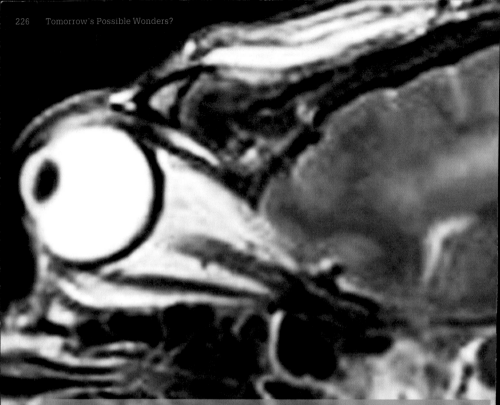

One single gram of DNA can hold around 500 petabytes of data. Storing this amount of data in a super small liquid substance is impressive, but still minuscule compared to the order of magnitude at which nature handles information. The maximum volume of information that the implanted brain processor can handle is 295 exabytes, which is equivalent to 0.59 l of extra liquid circulating around the human body.

The capacity of the Super Library (Bio-Net) is still a tiny fraction (less than 1 per cent) of the data that all the DNA molecules of human beings contain. The natural world is mind-boggling when it comes to data storage and processing capacities. By contrast, the world's technological information processing capacities might be growing at exponential rates, but are based on electrical engineering and silicon, which led to the production of finite storage systems such as CDs and hard drives. The Super Library is a pioneering form of biological engineering and augments human knowledge by treating human DNA as another 'digital' storage device.

Besides storing information, synthetic DNA is also capable of harvesting information from the body and senses while circulating around the human body: it can monitor the senses and emotions, thus generating a thorough understanding of empirical data. Medical care has never been so efficient: the life expectancy of humans has been extended to an average of 150 years.

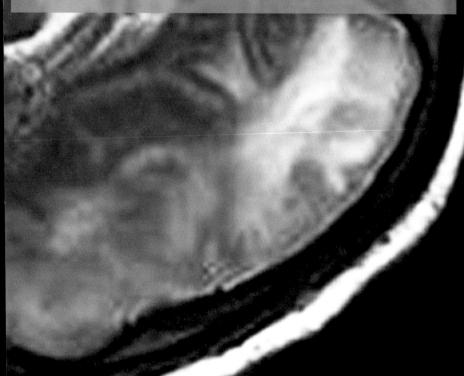

The Super Library exchanges information by touching the person with whom one wants to exchange information. This raises the question of who controls this information and what they can access. Could these human 'servers' be hacked? At what level is this information lethal? Designed hallucinations allow people to access the stored data. All someone needs to do is close his or her eyes and think of something, which activates the storage and provides access to the data. Mind control makes it possible to browse through the data and select it for access.

Scientists were developing a Retinal Eye Projection (REP) system, which they thought would be a means to access stored information. However, they found that designed hallucinations familiar from experiments with drugs such as LSD and from patients suffering from serious schizophrenia could solve the technical problem of selecting and accessing the data. Scientists managed to design an artificial neural network that allows for data access from the processor and activates and interferes with the network that generates output for images.

The creation of the omnipresent super library changes everything in our societies: politics, justice, economics, medicine, health care, food industry, construction methods, transportation, trade, banking, etcetera. The whole architecture of society will be transformed, there will be an enormous increase in individual self-organization, people will probably unite to fight the biggest and most universal problem of humankind, that of death.

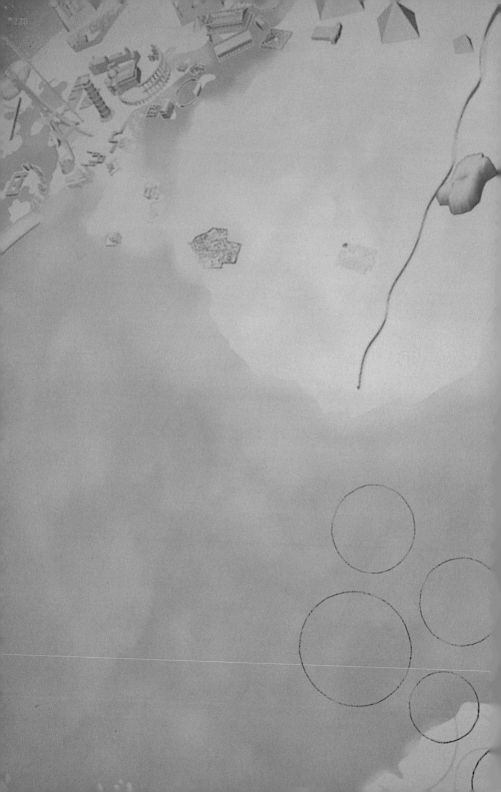

# Do We Need New Architectural Myths?

## Epilogue

Tihamér Salij

'Is it folly to believe in
something that is intangible?
After all, some of the greatest
intangibles are Love, Hope, and
Wonder. Another is Deity.
The choice to be a fool is yours.'

Vera Nazarian (Russian-born American writer, b. 1966)

Architectural wonders keep reminding us of how creative and inventive we are. They challenge and renew our wonderment with the world and continue to push the creative ability of humankind beyond unimagined limits. Man-made world wonders are custodians of our legacy of survival in a cruel world that is dominated by uncertainties. With their advanced technologies they feed human progress and provide evidence of ingenuity. They unite and propagate a collective sense of confidence, unity, joy and universal beauty. They indicate new directions for our futures, restore our faith and offer a hopeful glimpse of certainty. They are pioneers in science and smart technologies, embody record-breaking sizes, and tell great stories about fear, love, death, survival and hope. They speak to our collective longing for truth, goodness, harmony and evolution on the road to enlightenment.

Besides being important social and cultural assets, man-made world wonders are sources of innovation and inspiration and have a great impact on the broader economy. Investment in creating more man-made world wonders is important because they

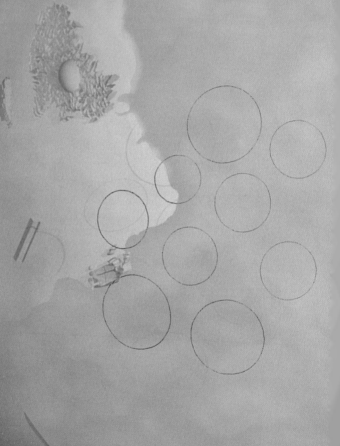

are key to the activation of regional and global social mobility. They directly contribute to regional and national productivity and are responsible for thousands of jobs in formal as well as informal economies. In combination with the social mobility and the cultural and economic exchange that this generates, world wonders create more jobs and generate more revenue than a conventional manufacturing plant or a major office of a global brand.

Architecture has become more than the mere production of functional buildings; it has become the making of supernatural places, of contexts, of social networks and new beliefs including environmental and social responsibilities, as well as of new societies and ecologies. It makes use of the smartest materials, such as cutting-edge foams, coatings, metals, artificial DNA, bits and bytes, molecules and atoms, to make our homes, vehicles, gadgets and entire cities more efficient, flexible, adaptive, environmentally friendly and comfortable.
Our concepts of society, science and

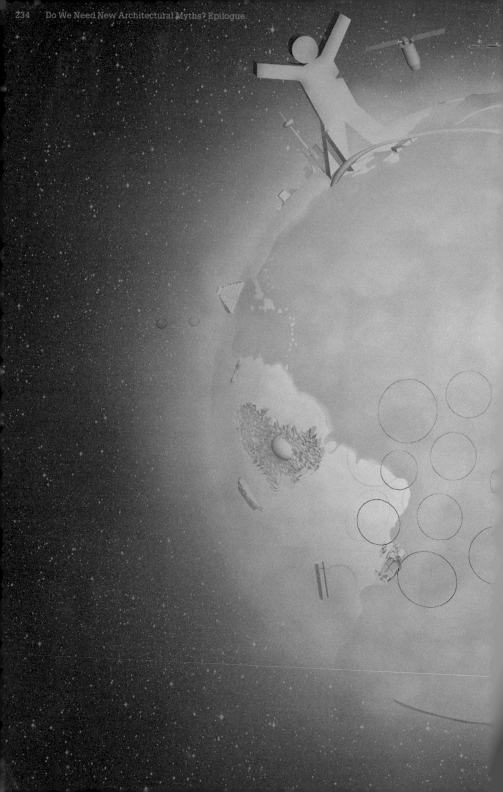

technology are, along with the ever-changing challenges presented by nature, the germinal seeds from which new world wonders are born, new myths formed, new realities forged and new architecture created.

There is a call for architecture to become more experimental, an integration of pioneering sciences, great storytelling and new scales, in order to meet the twenty-first century's social, spatial and environmental responsibilities and desires and make new myths a reality.

# Authors and Credits

# Authors

**Winy Maas** Prof. Ir. Ing. FRIBA, HAIA, Chevalier (b. 1959, Schijndel, the Netherlands) is an architect and urban designer. He is one of the co-founding directors of the globally operating architecture and urban planning firm MVRDV, based in Rotterdam, the Netherlands, known for buildings such as the Dutch Pavilion at the Expo 2000 in Hannover, the hanging houses in Amsterdam, the VPRO building in Hilversum and urban plans such as the urban plan for Eindhoven Flight Forum and the vision for greater Paris, Grand Paris Plus Petit.

He is professor of architecture and urban planning at Delft University of Technology. He is director of The Why Factory, the research institute for the future city that he founded in 2008 at Delft University of Technology, which collaborates with other institutes, such as the HKU in HongKong, the IIT in Chicago, the ETH in Zurich and the Strelka Institute in Moscow.

Before this he was, among other things, professor at the Berlage Institute in Rotterdam, the Massachusetts Institute of Technology in Boston, Ohio State University in Columbus and Yale University in New Haven.
He is supervisor of urban development and master plans in Almere, Bordeaux, Caen, Mannheim, Basel, Johannesburg and Oslo. Current projects include various building projects in Europe, the Americas, Africa and Asia.

With both MVRDV and The Why Factory, Maas has published a series of books.

More information at: www.mvrdv.nl and www.thewhyfactory.com

**Tihamér Salij** (1974, Ede, The Netherlands) is a researcher, architect and artist. He is founding director of Space Intelligence Agency (S.I.A.), an architecture and urban research and design practice based in Rotterdam, specialized in socially responsible city development, architecture and storytelling. S.I.A. was the editor of the publication *NL 28 – Olympic Fire* and co-curator of the exhibition in Rotterdam (NL) of the same title.

Tihamér Salij was a lecturer at the Academy of Technology and Innovation in Amersfoort and Utrecht and the coordinator of the Media Faculty. He worked at the architecture office MVRDV as a researcher and editor. Projects he worked on include The Region Maker, Rhine Ruhr City and Pig City. He co-curated the exhibition 'Rhine Ruhr City' in Düsseldorf (GER) and co-edited the publication *KM3 – Excursions on Capacity*.

Tihamér Salij has been a visiting lecturer at various universities worldwide such as the Chinese Academy of Fine Arts (CAFA) in Beijing, the Hong Kong University (HKU) and the Chinese University of Hong Kong (CUHK) in Hong Kong, the Berlage Institute in Rotterdam. He has written numerous articles on a wide range of topics. With his experience and expertise in futuring methodologies, scenario making, parametric modeling and performance-oriented design Tihamér Salij currently conducts research and teaches within the Future City Program at Delft University of Technology, where he has been affiliated with The Why Factory since 2007.

More information can be found at:
www.thewhyfactory.com, bk.tudelft.nl and www.spaceintelligenceagency.eu.

# Sources

[1] http://www.touregypt.net/featurestories/pyramidworkforce.htm (accessed August 21, 2014)

[2] http://learningenglish.voanews.com/content/a-23-2006-12-12-voa1-83131482/126717.html (accessed June 3, 2014)

[3] http://learningenglish.voanews.com/content/a-23-2006-12-12-voa1-83131482/126717.html (accessed June 3, 2014)

[4] http://whc.unesco.org/en/list/ (accessed August 28, 2014)

[5] http://www.askamathematician.com/2012/08/q-if-you-could-drill-a-tunnel-through-the-whole-planet-and-then-jumped-down-this-tunnel-how-would-you-fall/ (accessed June 3, 2014)

[6] In 2004, GeoDelft, together with the TU Delft and contractor Volker Wessels (and, during the later stages, the French contractor Soletanche Bachy) conducted research into BioGrout: the biological soil improvement method.

# Credits

Book Concept and Editors: Winy Maas and Tihamér Salij
Developmental Editor: Andrew May
Research Assistants: Francesco Vedovato, Maria
Lisogorskaya, Stavros Gargaretas, Lila Athanasiadou,
Denisa Annová, Mila Dimitrovska

Publication Manager: Tihamér Salij
With special thanks to Jennifer Sigler.

All projects presented in this book are based on the
material produced during The Why Factory's first-year
Master's studios called 'New World Wonders' at Delft
University of Technology in 2008 and 2011.

This book was made possible thanks to the generous
support of the New7Wonders Foundation in Zurich.

New World Wonders (1)
Masters studio at The Why Factory at the Faculty of
Architecture of Delft University of Technology, February
– June 2008.

Tutors: Winy Maas, Tihamér Salij, Young Wook Joung,
Daliana Suryawinata
Critics: Deborah Hauptmann, Patrick Healy,
Bernard Weber
Students: Peter Bednar, Alessandro Bua, Qing Chen,
Valerio Ciotola, Nicolas Fabre, Raul Forsoni,
Andrea Guazzieri, Diederik de Koning, Ahmet Korfalÿ,
Emilie Meaud, Hansol Moon, Dongho Nam,
Andreia Peñaloza Caicedo, Deniza Radulova, Qian Ren,
Hyun Soo Suh, Qili Yang.

New World Wonders (2)
Masters studio at The Why Factory at the Faculty
of Architecture of Delft University of Technology,
September 2010 – January 2011

Tutors: Winy Maas, Tihamér Salij, Daliana Suryawinata
Students: Ilkka Ala-Fossi, Zhou Bo, Isabella Eriksson,
Seung-min Ko, Yilun Pan, Garyfalia Pitsaki, Michael
Schuurman, Stavros Kousoulas, Douwe Strating, Manuel
Torres, Philip van der Linden, Mischa-Marah Wullems.

## Text Authors:
We Want World Wonders. Introduction: Winy Maas
Is There a Desire for World Wonders?: Tihamér Salij
What Makes a Man-Made World Wonder?: Tihamér Salij
Tomorrow's Possible Wonders?: Tihamér Salij

## Project Authors:
The Face on the Moon: Ilkka Ala-Fossi (original title:
Faces of the moon)
The String: Ahmet Korfalÿ (original title:
Ark of Extinction)
The Global Asteroid Protection Shield:
Philip van der Linden (original title: Echelon 8)

The Space Transport System: Michael Schuurman
(original title: The Space Experience)
The Typhoon Controller: Hansol Moon
The Third Life Centre: Alessandro Bua
The Wonder Walkways: Seung-min Ko, Isabella Eriksson
The Planted City: Philip van der Linden (original title:
City of Flowers)
The Floating Gardens: Diederik de Koning (original title:
The Well-Tempered City)
The Uplifted Islands: Yilun Pan (original title:
The Armada of the Maldives), Douwe Strating
(original title: The Garbage Collector)
The Global Shortcut: Deniza Radulova
The War Zone: Nicolas Fabre and Raul Forsoni
The Organ Farm: Seung-min Ko (original title:
The Valley of Belly), Philip van der Linden (original title:
The Evergrowth)
The Colossus: Peter Bednar (original title:
The Very Iconic Building)
The Long Span: Michael Schuurman (original title:
The Tube)
The Leaning Building: Mischa-Marah Wullems
(original title: The Staircase Tower)
The Artificial Sun: Diederik de Koning
The Dancing Cloud: Chen Qing (original title:
Universal Religious Centre)
The Needle: The Why Factory
Invisible Buildings: Isabella Eriksson (original title:
The Other Dimension)
The Secluded Desert: Isabella Eriksson (original title:
The Largest Performing Wall), Seung-min Ko
(original title: The Green Maker) both inspired by
'The Great Green Wall Initiative' by The African Union
The Lightning Harvester: Manuel Torres
The Super Library: The Why Factory: Tihamér Salij

Do We Need New Architectural Myths? Epilogue:
Tihamér Salij

Copy Editor: D'Laine Camp
Graphic Design: www.beng.nl
Design of The Why Factory logo: Thonik in collaboration
with studio BENG
Lithography and Printing: Die Keure, Bruges (B)
Paper: Arctic Volume, 120 grs
Publisher: Marcel Witvoet, nai010 publishers, Rotterdam

nai010 publishers is an internationally orientated publisher specialized in developing, producing and distributing books in the fields of architecture, urbanism, art and design.
www.nai010.com

North, Central and South America - Artbook | D.A.P., New York, USA, dap@dapinc.com

Rest of the world - Idea Books, Amsterdam, the Netherlands, idea@ideabooks.nl

For general questions, please contact nai010 publishers directly at sales@nai010.com or visit our website www.nai010.com for further information.

Printed and bound in Belgium
ISBN 9 789462 081772